Essential Barcelona

AAA Publishing 1000 AAA Drive, Heathrow, Florida 32746

Barcelona: Regions and Best places to see

★ Best places to see 36–55

■ Featured sight

Las Ramblas and around 85–112

La Ribera to Port Olímpic 113–126

The Eixample and Gràcia 127–146

Montjuïc to Sants 147–154

Pedralbes and Tibidabo 155–161

Original text by Teresa Fisher
Revised and updated by Lucy Ratcliffe

Edited, designed and produced by AA Publishing
© AA Media Limited 2011

AA Media Limited retains the copyright in the original edition © 1999 and in all subsequent editions, reprints and amendments.

All rights reserved. No part of this publication may be reproduced, stored in a retrieval system, or transmitted in any form or by any means – electronic, photocopying, recording or otherwise – unless the written permission of the publishers has been obtained beforehand.

The contents of this publication are believed correct at the time of printing. Nevertheless, the publishers cannot be held responsible for any errors or omissions or for changes in the details given in this guide or for the consequences of any reliance on the information provided by the same.

Published in the United States by AAA Publishing,
1000 AAA Drive, Heathrow, Florida 32746.
Published in the United Kingdom by AA Publishing.

978-1-59508-413-2

Color separation: AA Digital Department
Printed and bound in Italy by Printer Trento S.r.l.

A04658
Maps in this title produced from mapping © MAIRDUMONT/Falk Verlag 2011
Transport map © Communicarta Ltd, UK

About this book

Symbols are used to denote the following categories:

- map reference to maps on cover
- address or location
- telephone number
- opening times
- admission charge
- restaurant or cafe on premises or nearby
- nearest underground train station
- nearest bus/tram route
- nearest overground train station
- nearest ferry stop
- nearest airport
- tourist information office
- other practical information
- ➤ indicates the page where you will find a fuller description

This book is divided into six sections.

The essence of Barcelona pages 6–19
Introduction; Features; Food and drink; Short break

Planning pages 20–33
Before you go; Getting there; Getting around; Being there

Best places to see pages 34–55
The unmissable highlights of any visit to Barcelona

Best things to do pages 56–81
Great cafes; Stunning views; Places to take the children and more

Exploring pages 82–161
The best places to visit in Barcelona, organized by area

Excursions pages 162–182
Places to visit out of town

Maps
All map references are to the maps on the covers. For example, Casa Milà has the reference 8F – indicating the grid square in which it is to be found.

Admission prices
Inexpensive (under €4)
Moderate (€4–€9)
Expensive (over €9)

Hotel prices
Prices are per room per night:
€ budget (under €110);
€€ moderate (€110–€180);
€€€ expensive to luxury (over €180)

Restaurant prices
Price for a three-course meal per person without drinks:
€ budget (under €25);
€€ moderate (€25–€50);
€€€ expensive (over €50)

Contents

THE ESSENCE OF...

6 – 19

PLANNING

20 – 33

BEST PLACES TO SEE

34 – 55

BEST THINGS TO DO

56 – 81

EXPLORING...

82 – 161

EXCURSIONS

162 – 182

The essence of...

Introduction 8–9

Features 10–11

Food and drink 12–15

Short break 16–19

Barcelona is unique. It has something for everyone and is one of Europe's top destinations. The only problem you will encounter is that there will never be enough time to explore its many museums and monuments, churches and galleries, its fascinating coastline and its delectable cuisine.

To enjoy your stay to the fullest, you will need to adopt the Barcelonan lifestyle – a striking blend of businesslike efficiency combined with long alfresco lunches, lazy siestas, ritual evening promenades and an intoxicating nightlife. You will long remember its proud yet generous people, who will welcome you back with open arms when you return, as you surely will.

features

Inventive and innovative, radical and racy, Barcelona is one of Europe's most dynamic cities. Strolling through its streets is like wandering through a living museum, a legacy of its remarkable 2,000 years of history. From the ancient maze-like Gothic quarter, built within the Roman city walls, to the astonishing regimental grid plan of the turn-of-the-19th-century Eixample district, studded with eye-catching jewels of Modernista architecture, and the space-age constructions for the 1992 Olympics, the city contains some of the finest and most eccentric art and architecture in the world. Outstanding even by Barcelonan standards is Gaudí's extraordinary Sagrada Família – reason enough to visit the city.

Just as *Modernisme* – the movement that has made Barcelona unique – emerged at the end of the 19th century as a desire for change and renovation, so today the city is celebrating its past.

It is restoring its old buildings, introducing new art and architecture and eradicating some severe urban problems, while staying at the forefront of contemporary culture. As a result, Barcelona today is very much alive – a city bursting with new pride and self-confidence, which cannot fail to excite and delight.

GEOGRAPHY

● Barcelona is in northeastern Spain, 166km (103 miles) from the French border. The city occupies 99sq km (62sq miles), with 13km (8 miles) of Mediterranean coastline, including 4km (2.5 miles) of sandy beaches. It is bounded by the mountains of Montjuïc (to the south) and Tibidabo (to the northwest), and framed by the rivers Llobregat (to the south) and Besós (to the north).

PEOPLE AND ECONOMY

● Barcelona's population is 1,673,075 (or 3,161,081 within the *area metropolitana* of greater Barcelona). Many inhabitants originated from southern Spain, drawn to Catalonia in the 1950s and 1960s by the prospect of work in the capital of Spain's most progressive and prosperous region.

BARCELONA FOR WHEELCHAIR USERS

● Barcelona is a compact city so is a popular destination for wheelchair users, and the modern attractions are wheelchair-friendly. However, many streets are cobbled, which can be uncomfortable unless appropriate tyres are fitted. The city's buses, including the *Bus Turístic* have low-entry doors and wheelchair points and all buses are wheelchair accessible. Many, but not all, of the major metro stations are adapted to be suitable for wheelchairs.

CATALUNYA (CATALONIA)

● The autonomous region of Catalunya (Catalonia) covers an area of 32,114sq km (12,396sq miles) (6.3 per cent of Spain) and has a population of 7.5 million (16 per cent of the Spanish population), 60 per cent of whom live in greater Barcelona. It is Spain's leading economic region, producing 18 per cent of the country's gross national product. Nearly 25 per cent of visitors to Spain come to Catalonia.

food & drink

No one visiting Barcelona should leave without trying its cuisine, described by the American food critic Colman Andrews as "the last great culinary secret in Europe". Rooted in the fresh local ingredients of the mountains, the plains and sea, the food is delicious and suprisingly subtle in flavour.

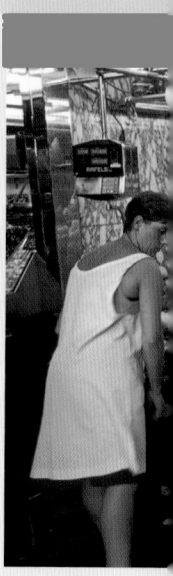

MEDITERRANEAN FLAVOURS

The main ingredients of traditional Catalan dishes are typically Mediterranean: tomatoes, garlic, olive oil, aubergines (eggplant), courgettes (zucchini), peppers and herbs, which, when blended, form *samfaina*, a delicious sauce served with many dishes. Other principal sauces include *picada* (nuts, bread, parsley, garlic and saffron), *sofregit* (a simple sauce of onion, tomato and garlic lightly fried in olive oil) and *allioli* (a strong, garlicky mayonnaise).

For centuries *llom* (pork) has been the cornerstone of the Catalan diet. Little is wasted – even the *peus de porc* (pigs' trotters) are considered a delicacy. No bar would be complete without its haunch of *pernil* (cured ham), a popular tapas dish, and you often see a variety of *butifarra* (sausages) hanging from the rafters of restaurants and delicatessens. Lamb, chicken, duck, beef and

game also feature strongly, often prepared *a la brasa* (on an open charcoal grill) and served with a large serving of *allioli* (garlic mayonnaise).

MAR I MUNTANYA

In Catalan cuisine, meat is commonly combined with fruit, creating such mouth-watering dishes as *pollastre amb pera* (chicken with pears) and *conill amb prunes* (rabbit with prunes). However, it is the unique "surf'n'turf" combinations that sea and mountain *(Mar i Muntanya)* produce which differentiates Catalan cuisine from the cookery of other Spanish regions. *Sépia amb mandonguilles* (cuttlefish with meatballs) and *mar i cel* ("sea and heaven" – made with sausages, rabbit, shrimp and fish) are especially tasty.

Near the coast, fish dishes reign supreme, ranging from simple grilled *sardinas* (sardines) and hearty *zarsuela* (seafood stew) to eye-catching

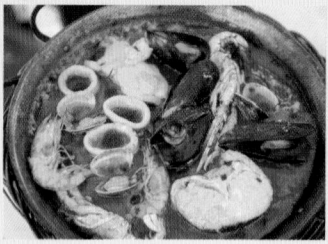

shellfish displays. Try *suquet de peix* (fish and potato soup) or the more unusual *broudegos* ("dog soup") made with fish, onions and orange juice, followed by speciality dishes *arròs negre* (rice cooked in black squid ink), *fideuá* (a local variant of paella, using vermicelli and noodles and not rice) or *bacallà* (salt cod), which comes *a la llauna* (with garlic, tomato and white wine), *esqueixada* (a salt cod and black olive salad), *amb samfaina* or *amb romesco* (a piquant sauce, made from a mixture of crushed nuts, tomatoes and spicy red pepper).

FINE WINES

A short distance south of Barcelona, the Penedès is the main Catalan wine region, producing quality red *(negre)*, white *(blanc)* and rosé *(rosat)* wines. Look for the reliable Torres, Masia Bach and René Barbier labels. Catalan *cava* (sparkling wine) also comes from the Penedès wineries, made by the *méthode champenoise*. Famous names include Freixenet and Codorníu, which can be sampled in the cava bars of Barcelona. To the north, the Alella and Empordà regions produce white wines, while Priorat produces excellent, heavy reds.

short break

If you have only a short time to visit Barcelona and would like to take home some unforgettable memories, you can do something local and capture the real flavour of the city. The following suggestions will give you a wide range of sights and experiences that won't take very long, won't cost very much and will make your visit very special. If you only have time to choose just one of these, you will have found the true heart of the city.

- **Stroll along Las Ramblas** (➤ 50–51), pause for a coffee and enjoy the street performers.

- **Get into Gaudí**, especially Casa Milà (La Pedrera) (➤ 36–37), Park Güell (➤ 48–49) and the famous La Sagrada Família (➤ 52–53).

- **Follow in the footsteps** of Picasso and Dalí and wander at length through the maze of narrow streets in the Barri Gòtic (➤ 72–73, 86–88).

BAR
RESTAURANT

DIONISES

- **Enjoy the wide variety** of tapas (➤ 60–61) available in the local bars.
- **Watch locals dance** the *sardana*, the national dance of Catalonia (➤ 39).
- **Experience the tastes**, fragrances and colours of the Mediterranean at Mercat de la Boqueria (➤ 66).
- **Visit the Museu Picasso** (➤ 46–47).
- **Shop for Spanish fashion** and designer gifts in the smart Eixample district (➤ 142–145).
- **Watch FC Barça** play a home match (➤ 156).
- **Walk the waterfront** and sample the freshest of seafood (➤ 114–115).

Planning

Before you go 22–25

Getting there 26–27

Getting around 27–29

Being there 29–33

L3
Zona Universitària
Sortida
Portal de Sta Madrona

Before you go

WHEN TO GO

JAN	FEB	MAR	APR	MAY	JUN	JUL	AUG	SEP	OCT	NOV	DEC
14°C	15°C	17°C	19°C	22°C	25°C	29°C	29°C	27°C	23°C	18°C	15°C
57°F	59°F	62°F	66°F	72°F	77°F	84°F	84°F	80°F	73°F	64°F	59°F

High season Low season

The temperatures given in the chart above are the average daily maximum for each month. The best time to visit Barcelona is May to June or September to October, when the weather is fine but not too hot, and there is a lot going on in the city. July and August see an exodus of locals and many museums, restaurants and shops either close or reduce their opening hours; day-trippers from coastal resorts crowd the city; and the weather can be hot and sticky, with some violent thunderstorms. On the upside, there are a handful of fiestas and festivals to keep you entertained. Winters are cool but seldom cold, and it rarely snows; when skies are blue and visibility perfect, January and February can be good months of the year.

WHAT YOU NEED

● Required
○ Suggested
▲ Not required

Some countries require a passport to remain valid for a minimum period (usually at least six months) beyond the date of entry – check before you travel.

	UK	Germany	USA	Canada	Australia	Ireland	Netherlands	Spain
Passport (or National Identity Card where applicable)	●	●	●	●	●	●	●	●
Visa (regulations can change – check before you travel)	▲	▲	▲	▲	▲	▲	▲	▲
Onward or Return Ticket	▲	▲	▲	▲	▲	▲	▲	▲
Health Inoculations (tetanus and polio)	▲	▲	▲	▲	▲	▲	▲	▲
Health Documentation (➤ 23, Health insurance)	●	●	●	●	●	●	●	●
Travel Insurance	○	○	○	○	○	○	○	○
Driving Licence (national)	●	●	●	●	●	●	●	●
Car Insurance Certificate	○	○	n/a	n/a	n/a	○	○	○
Car Registration Document	●	●	n/a	n/a	n/a	●	●	●

WEBSITES

City Council of Barcelona
www.bcn.es

Tourist Authority
www.barcelonaturisme.com

TOURIST OFFICES AT HOME

In the UK
Spanish Tourist Office
22–23 Manchester Square
London W1U 3PX
☎ 020 7486 8077

In the US (New York)
Tourist Office of Spain
666 Fifth Avenue, 35th Floor
New York, NY 10103
☎ 212 265-8822

In Germany
Kurfürstendamm 63, 5.OG
10707 Berlin
☎ 030 882 65 43

In the US (Los Angeles)
Tourist Office of Spain
8383 Wilshire Blvd, Suite 960
Beverly Hills, CA 90211
☎ 323 658-7188

HEALTH INSURANCE

Nationals of EU countries can obtain medical treatment at reduced cost with the relevant documentation (EHIC – European Health Insurance Card), although private medical insurance is still advised and is essential for all other visitors.

Dental treatment is not free of charge. A list of *dentistas* can be found in the yellow pages. Dental treatment should be covered by private medical insurance.

TIME DIFFERENCES

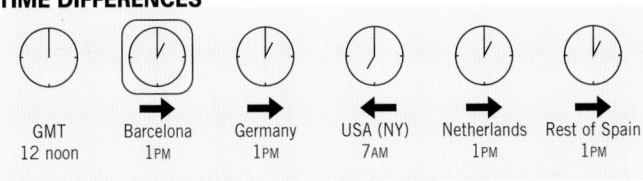

Like the rest of Spain, Catalonia is one hour ahead of Greenwich Mean Time (GMT+1), except from late March to late October, when summer time (GMT+2) operates.

NATIONAL HOLIDAYS

1 Jan *New Year's Day*
6 Jan *Three King's*
19 Mar *Sant Josep*
Mar/Apr *Good Friday and Easter Monday*
1 May *Labour Day*
May/Jun *Whit Sunday*
24 Jun *St John*
15 Aug *Assumption Day*
11 Sep *Catalan National Day*
24 Sep *Our Lady of Mercy*
12 Oct *Hispanitat*
1 Nov *All Saints' Day*
6 Dec *Constitution Day*
8 Dec *Feast of the Immaculate Conception*
25 Dec *Christmas Day*
26 Dec *Sant Esteve*

Most banks, businesses, museums and shops are closed on these days.

WHAT'S ON WHEN

The venues and events listed here are liable to change from one year to the next and, in the case of major festivals, there is often more than one venue. Dates may also vary slightly from year to year.

January *Reis Mags* (6 Jan): the Three Kings (Melchior, Caspar and Balthasar) arrive by boat at the bottom of Las Ramblas the night before, then tour the city with a retinue of acrobats and circus clowns, showering the waiting crowds with sweets.

February *Santa Eulàlia* (12–19 Feb): a series of cultural and musical events in honour of one of the city's patron saints.
Carnestoltes: one week of pre-Lenten carnival celebrations and costumed processions comes to an end on Ash Wednesday with the symbolic burial of a sardine.

March *Sant Medir de Gràcia* (3 Mar): procession of traditionally dressed horsemen from Gràcia who ride over Collserola to the Hermitage of Sant Medir (Saint of Broad Beans) for a bean-feast.

March/April *Setmana Santa:* religious services and celebrations for Easter Week include solemn processions.

April *Sant Jordi* (23 Apr): Catalonia's most revered celebration when streets are thronging with rose and book sellers in honour of Saint George. Most museums and sights are free on this day.

June *Midsummer* (23–24 Jun) is a good excuse for partying and fireworks.
El Grec (end Jun–Aug): Barcelona's biggest arts festival with top names in music and theatre performing nightly.

July *Aplec de la Sardana*, Olot (2nd Sunday): the biggest *Sardana* dancing festival in Catalonia.

August *Festa Major de Gràcia* (3rd week of Aug): a popular festival of music, dancing and street celebrations in the Gràcia district (► 131).

September *Diada de Catalunya* (11 Sep): Catalonia's National Day is in memory of all the martyrs for the nation of Catalonia and solemnly marks the taking of the city by Felipe V in 1714.
La Mercè (19–25 Sep): parades featuring giants, devils, dragons, big heads and fireworks, and free outdoor concerts.
Festa Major de la Barceloneta (last week of Sep): a lively district *feste*, with processions and dancing in the streets every night.

October *International Jazz Festival*: draws many international names.

December *Christmas festivities* (end Nov–23 Dec): include a craft fair and trees outside the cathedral and a crib in Plaça Sant Jaume.

For more information about all the city's festivals while you are in Barcelona check out www.bcn.es, dial 010 (city hall information line), or visit the cultural information centre,
La Palau de la Virreina, Las Ramblas 99.

Getting there

BY AIR

El Prat de Llobregat Airport

7km (4.3 miles) to city centre

25 minutes

20 minutes

15 minutes

Spain's national airline, Iberia, has scheduled flights to Barcelona's El Prat de Llobregat Airport from major Spanish and European cities. The city is served by over 30 international airlines and has direct flights to more than 80 international destinations. Non-stop flights are operated from New York by Iberia, in association with its partner in the Oneworld alliance, American Airlines. Most flights from North America involve a stop at Madrid or one of the other leading European airports, although Continental and Delta Airlines also fly non-stop to Barcelona from several US airports. From the UK and Ireland the lowest fares are often on no-frills airlines. These include easyJet, from Gatwick, Luton and Stansted and Ryan Air which flies from Stansted and Luton to Girona (80km/50 miles north of Barcelona) from where there is a bus to Barcelona. British Airways and its alliance partner, Iberia, fly from Gatwick, Heathrow, Birmingham and Manchester. British Midland (bmi) flies from Heathrow, and easyJet also flies from Liverpool. Iberia flies from Dublin, in association with its Oneworld partner Aer Lingus. There are no direct flights to Spain from Australia or New Zealand; connections via London, Frankfurt or Paris are the most common. Approximate flying times to Barcelona: London (1.5 hours), Liverpool (2 hours), New York (8 hours).

Flight prices tend to be highest in spring and summer (Easter to September). Check with airlines, travel agents, tour operators and the internet for the current best deals.

BY RAIL

The main regional, national and international rail station is Sants-Estació. Comfortable, fast, express trains connect the city to Paris, Madrid and Valencia and other destinations in Europe.

BY ROAD

The AP7 highway connects the French border with Barcelona, a distance of only 166km (103 miles), though tolls are expensive. The AP2 connects the Spanish capital of Madrid with Barcelona, a distance of 660km (410 miles); most of the trip is also via toll roads. Well-paved and lit multi-lane toll roads are common all over Catalonia, and although free *carreteras nacionales* provide alternatives, they are busier and generally less safe owing to poorer surfaces and lighting.

Getting around

PUBLIC TRANSPORT

Metro The metro is the easiest and fastest way of moving around the city. There are two different underground train systems, the metro with its six lines identified by number and colour, and the FGC, an older service which is above ground in outer Barcelona. Both lines have been integrated into the same system (visit www.tmb.net for more information).

Buses Barcelona has an excellent bus network; pick up a free plan from any tourist office (or download from www.tmb.net). Timetables are also shown at individual bus stops. Buses run 6am–10pm. At night there is a *Nitbus* with routes centred on Plaça de Catalunya. Throughout the year the *Bus Turístic*, a hop-on, hop-off service, circuits the main city sights.

Trains The Spanish railway system, RENFE (www.renfe.com), runs trains from Barcelona to all the major cities in Spain. Many mainline trains stop at the underground stations at Passeig de Gràcia and Plaça de Catalunya. There are three main railway stations: Estació de Sants and Estació de França near Barceloneta, and Passeig de Gràcia in the Eixample.

Boat The best way to admire the port and coastline is from the sea. *Golondrinas* offer 35-minute harbour tours or 2-hour voyages along the beaches to Port Forum. Barcelona is the biggest Mediterranean port, with regular passenger services to the Balearic islands and to Genoa and Rome.

Cable cars, funiculars and trams A spectacular cable car connects the lower city with Montjuïc castle and links with the funicular railway. To reach Tibidabo, take the FGC to the Peu de Funicular station, then the Funicular del Tibidabo to the Amusement Park at the top of the hill.

TAXIS

Pick up a black and yellow taxi at a taxi rank or hail one if it's displaying a green light and the sign *Lliure/Libre* (free). Fares are not unduly expensive but extra fees are charged for airport trips and for baggage, and at weekends and after 8:30pm. Supplements are shown on a sticker inside and prices on the meter.

DRIVING

- Drive on the right.
- Speed limits on motorways *(autopistas)*: 120kph/74mph; on main roads: 100kph/62mph; on minor roads: 90kph/56mph; in towns *(Poblaciones)*: 50kph/31mph.
- Seat belts must be worn at all times where fitted.
- Random breath-testing takes place. Never drive under the influence of alcohol.
- Fuel *(gasolina)* is available as: unleaded or *sin plomo* (90 octane), *gasoleo* or *gasoil* (diesel). *Super* (96 octane) is being phased out. Fuel stations are normally open 6am–10pm, though larger ones are open 24 hours. All take credit cards.

CAR RENTAL

The leading international car rental companies have offices at Barcelona airport and in the town centre. The local outfit Pepecar (www.pepecar.com) also has competitive prices and several central locations. In peak periods make sure you reserve a car in advance

FARES AND CONCESSIONS

Travel cards (*targetas*) come in options of 2 to 5 days or for 10 journeys (T-10) and are available from all metro stations. They are valid for metro, FGC, bus and some overland (RENFE) trains; transfers (one change of mode of transport) are allowed. With *targetas*, you pay half the price (or less, depending on the amount of travel) of a single journey (€1.40).

The Barcelona Card, available from tourist offices, offers savings on museums, sights and and includes unlimited use of public transport. The cards are available in 2- to 5-day options (€26–€42). Barcelona *Bus Turistic* is a hop-on, hop-off bus with several routes covering all the sights. Tickets are available for unlimited travel over one or two days (€22–€29).

Holders of an International Student Identity Card (ISIC) or Euro 26 card may obtain some concessions on travel and entrance fees. Most museums offer 50 per cent discount to students, and many are free on Sunday afternoons after 3pm, others on the first Sunday of each month. There are several IYHF youth hostels in the city, with accommodation in multi-bed dormitories. Expect to pay around €20–€30 per person.

Most museums and galleries offer a 50 per cent discount on entrance fees to older people on production of photo ID or your passport.

Being there

TOURIST OFFICES

The main tourist office is situated beneath Plaça de Catalunya (and is well signposted). It provides a number of services including hotel reservations, currency exchange, walking tours and theatre and concert tickets.

There are branches of the city tourist office next to the city hall, at the Sants railway station and in front of the Columbus Monument (▶ 91).

There are also tourist information offices in the airport arrival halls, open daily 9–9.

- Turisme de Barcelona
Plaça de Catalunya 17
www.barcelonaturisme.com
☎ 93 28 538 34
Daily 9–9

- Plaça Sant Jaume I
Mon–Sat 9–8, Sun 10–2
Sants Railway Station (Estació de Sants)
Mon–Fri 8–8, Sat–Sun 8–2

- Turisme de Catalunya
Palau Robert
Passeig de Gràcia 107
www.gencat.net
☎ 93 238 80 91/012
Mon–Sat 10–7, Sun 10–2:30

In summer, information booths can be found at Sagrada Família and La Rambla. In the Barri Gòtic, you may also come across uniformed tourist officials, known as "Red Jackets".

MONEY

The euro (€) is the official currency of Spain. Banknotes are issued in denominations of €5, €10, €20, €50, €100, €200 and €500; coins are in denominations of 1, 2, 5, 10, 20 and 50 cents, and €1 and €2.

You can change traveller's cheques at banks and *caixes d'estalvis* (savings banks), at *oficines de canvi* (including late-night bureaux de change along Las Ramblas) and at stations and airports. Bureaux de change don't charge commission but apply less favourable rates.

Credit cards are widely accepted in shops, restaurants and hotels. All shops may require proof of identity such as ID card or passport (no copies). VISA, Mastercard and AMEX are the preferred cards, and they can be used to withdraw cash from widespread ATMs.

TIPS AND GRATUITIES

Yes ✓ No ✕		
Hotels (if service included)	✓	change
Restaurants	✓	5%
Cafes/bars	✓	change
Taxis	✓	change
Tour guides	✓	€1
Porters	✓	€1
Toilets	✕	

POSTAL AND INTERNET SERVICES

The main *Oficina Central* (post office) at Via Laietana 1 is open Mon–Sat 8:30am–9pm, and Sun 8–2. The Eixample post office at Carrer d'Aragó 282 is open Mon–Fri 8am–9pm and Sat 9–2pm. You can also buy stamps at any *estanc* (tobacconist).

WiFi internet access is becoming increasingly common in hotels and cafes. The cheapest internet access is found in *locutorios*, cheap call centres that are mainly clustered in El Raval neighbourhood. The biggest internet centre is easyEverything at Las Ramblas 31, open daily 8am–2:30am.

TELEPHONES

Increasingly, public phones require a phonecard *(tarjeta)*. You can buy these from post offices, news-stands and *estancs* (tobacconists).

Calls from phones in bars and cafes are more expensive than those made from phone booths on the street. The best place to make international calls is from *locutorios* (phone centres), chiefly found in the Raval district. International cheap rates apply from 8pm to 8am and all weekend. If you are travelling with your mobile phone, prepaid call time and SIM cards are available, provided you own a GSM, dual or triband cellular phone.

International dialling codes
Dial 00 followed by
UK: 44
USA/Canada: 1
Irish Republic: 353
Australia: 61
France: 33
Germany: 49

Emergency telephone numbers
City police (Policía Municipal): 092
National police (Policía nacional): 091
Fire (Bomberos): 080
Ambulance (Ambulància) 061

EMBASSIES AND CONSULATES

UK ☎ 93 366 62 00
Germany ☎ 93 292 10 00
USA ☎ 93 280 22 27
Netherlands ☎ 93 363 54 20
France ☎ 93 270 30 00

HEALTH ADVICE

Sun advice The sunniest (and hottest) months are July and August, with an average of 11 hours of sun a day and daytime temperatures of 29°C (84°F). Whatever the month, avoid midday sun and use a strong sunblock.
Pharmacies Prescription and non-prescription drugs and medicines are available from *farmàcias* (pharmacies), distinguished by a large green cross. They are able to dispense many drugs that would be available only on prescription in some other countries.
Safe water Tap water is generally safe though it can be heavily chlorinated. Mineral water is cheap to buy and is sold as *con gas* (carbonated) and *sin gas* (still). Drink plenty of water during hot weather.

PERSONAL SAFETY

The *Guardia Urbana*, who control traffic, wear navy and pale blue uniforms. Disturbances are dealt with by the *Mossos d' Escquadra* (navy uniform with red braid), the local Catalan police force. More serious crime is dealt with by the *Policia Nacional,* who also take *denuncias* (statements) in the case of robbery. To help prevent tourist-targeted petty crime:

- Do not carry more cash than you need.
- Do not leave valuables on the beach or poolside.
- Beware of pickpockets in crowded places.
- Avoid walking alone in dark alleys at night.
- Cars should be locked.

ELECTRICITY

The power supply is usually 220 volts but a few old buildings are still wired for 125 volts.

Sockets take two-round-pin-style plugs, so an adaptor is needed for most non-Continental appliances and a transformer for appliances operating on 110–120 volts.

OPENING HOURS

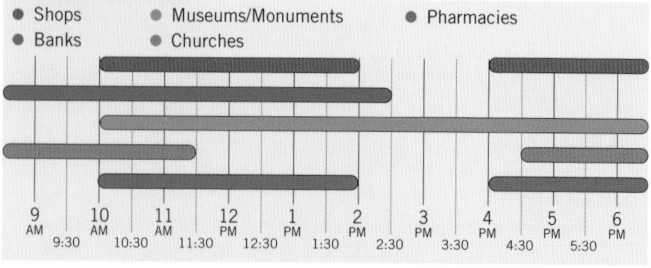

Large department stores and supermarkets may open outside these times, especially during the summer. Shops in the city centre don't close for lunch. Banks generally close on Saturdays, although main branches open in the morning 8:30–12:30. Outside banking hours, money-exchange facilities are available at the airport and Sants railway station. *Farmacias de Guardia* have extended opening hours. Some *barris* (districts) have their own feast days, when shops and offices may close.

LANGUAGE

In Barcelona, there are two official languages, Catalan and Spanish, both coming from Latin but both sounding quite different. Everybody can speak Spanish, although Catalan is more widely spoken. At most tourist sights you will always find someone who speaks English, and many restaurants have polyglot menus. However, it is advisable to try to learn at least some Catalan, since English is not widely spoken. Here is a basic vocabulary to help you with the most essential words and expressions.

yes	*si*	today	*avui*
no	*no*	tomorrow	*demà*
please	*per favor*	excuse me	*perdoni*
thank you	*gràcies*	how are you?	*com va?*
hello	*hola*	do you speak English?	*parla anglès?*
goodbye	*adéu*		
good morning	*bon dia*	I don't understand	*no ho enten*
good afternoon	*bona tarda*	how much?	*quant es?*
goodnight	*bona nit*	where is...?	*on és...?*
single room	*habitació senzilla*	bath	*bany*
double room	*habitació doble*	shower	*dutxa*
one night	*una nit*	toilet	*toaleta*
reservation	*reservas*	key	*clau*
room service	*servei d'habitació*	lift	*ascensor*
bank	*banc*	change	*camvi*
post office	*correos*	open	*obert*
credit card	*carta de crèdit*	closed	*tancat*
lunch	*dinar*	beer	*cervesa*
dinner	*sopar*	wine	*vi*
bill	*cuenta*	water	*aigua*
airport	*aeroport*	station	*estació*
train	*tren*	return ticket	*anar i tornar*
bus	*autobús*	non-smoking	*no fumar*

Best places to see

Casa Milà (La Pedrera)	36–37
Catedral	38–39
Fundació Joan Miró	40–41
Montjuïc	42–43
Museu Nacional d'Art de Catalunya (MNAC)	44–45
Museu Picasso	46–47
Parc Güell	48–49
Las Ramblas	50–51
La Sagrada Família	52–53
Santa Maria del Mar	54–55

1 Casa Milà (La Pedrera)

www.lapedreraeducacio.org

This apartment block is Gaudí's last and most famous secular building. Its roof terrace is an iconic image of the city.

Built between 1906 and 1912, Casa Milà, or La Pedrera, shows this great Catalan architect at his most inventive. It also shows Gaudí's genius as a structural engineer, with seven storeys built entirely on columns and arches, supposedly without a single straight line or right-angled corner. Its most distinctive features are the rippling limestone facade, with its intricate ironwork, and the strangely shaped chimneys of the roof terrace. In fact, the large amount of limestone is what gave rise to the building's common name of La Pedrera (the quarry).

A visit to La Pedrera includes the Espai Gaudí, a gallery about the architect's work, and the Pis de Pedrera, an apartment decorated as it was when the building contained private residences. The rooftop with its incredible views is a highlight.

8F Carrer Provença 261–265
90 240 09 73
Mar–Oct daily 9–8; Nov–Feb 9–6
Expensive
Diagonal 16, 17, 22, 24, 28 Audio-guide available

2 Catedral

www.catedralbcn.org

Barcelona's great cathedral is not only one of the most celebrated examples of Catalan Gothic style, but also one of the finest cathedrals in Spain.

The cathedral is located at the heart of the Barri Gòtic (► 72–73, 86–88), on the remains of an early Christian basilica. Most of the building was erected between the late 13th century and the middle of the 15th century, although the heavily ornate main facade and octagonal dome were constructed at the beginning of the 20th century.

The impressive interior represents a harmonious blend of medieval and Renaissance styles, with a lofty triple nave, graceful arches, 29 side chapels and an intricately carved choir. Beneath the main altar is the crypt of Santa Eulàlia (the patron saint of Barcelona), which contains her tomb.

Near the main entrance is the Chapel of Christ of Lepanto (formerly the Chapter House), which is widely considered to be the finest example of

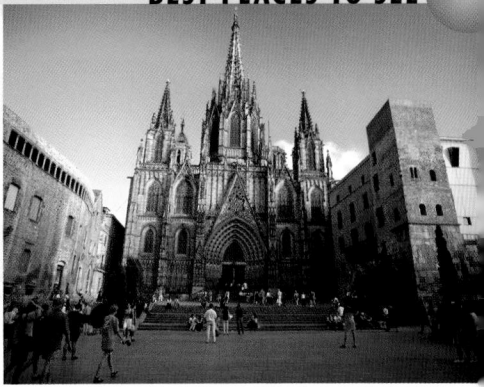

Gothic art in the cathedral. It contains the crucifix carried on board *La Real*, the flagship of Don Juan of Austria, during the famous Battle of Lepanto. The 14th-century cloister is the most beautiful part of the cathedral, its garden of magnolias, palms and fountains making a cool retreat. There is a small pond, with a flock of white geese, supposedly symbolizing Santa Eulàlia's virginal purity. A small **museum** just off the cloister shelters many of the cathedral's most precious treasures.

Despite its grandeur, the cathedral remains very much a people's church. The main entrance is on Plaça de la Seu and a side entrance along Carrer del Bisbe leads to the cloister. Worshippers outnumber tourists; on Sundays Barcelonans gather in Plaça de la Seu at noon to perform the *sardana*, Catalonia's stately national dance which symbolizes unity.

4c Plaça de la Seu 93 310 71 95
Mon–Fri 8–12:30, 5:15–7:30; VIP: daily 1–5
Free; roof inexpensive; VIP moderate Jaume I
17, 19, 40, 45 VIP entry also gives access to the roof and museum

Museum

Daily 10–6:45 Inexpensive Small gift shop

3 Fundació Joan Miró

www.bcn.fjmiro.es

This dazzling gallery pays homage to Joan Miró, one of Catalonia's greatest artists, famous for his childlike style and use of vibrant colours.

The Miró Foundation was set up by Joan Miró in 1971, and is devoted to the study of his works and to the promotion of contemporary art. The gallery – a modern building of white spaces, massive windows and skylights designed by Josep Lluís Sert – is itself a masterpiece and a perfect place in which to pursue the Foundation's aims. It contains some 240 of Miró's paintings, 175 sculptures, nine tapestries, his complete graphic works and more than 8,000 drawings, making it one of the world's most complete collections of this master.

Miró was born in Barcelona in 1893 and although, like many Catalan artists, he moved to Paris during the Civil War, his bold style of vigorous lines and intense primary colours owes much to the light and geography of Barcelona and Catalonia. In 1956 he moved to Mallorca, and remained on the island until his death in 1983.

Highlights of the gallery include some of Miró's earliest sketches, the tapestry *Tapis de la Fundació* and a set of black-and-white lithographs entitled *Barcelona Series* (1939–44) – an artistic appraisal of the war years. The roof terrace and gardens contain several striking sculptures.

The Foundation also presents temporary exhibitions of modern art, music recitals and a special permanent collection called "To Joan Miró", with works by Ernst, Tàpies, Calder and Matisse among others, a touching tribute to the person and his work.

16K Parc de Montjuïc 93 443 94 70 Oct–Jun Tue–Sat 10–7, Thu 10–9:30, Sun 10–2:30; Jul–Sep Tue–Sat 10–8, Thu 10–9:30, Sun 10–2:30 Moderate Cafe (€€) 50, 55, PM (Parc Monjuïc bus) Montjuïc funicular from Paral.lel Metro station

4 Montjuïc

Few can resist the charms of the city's local hill, with its splendid views, museums, galleries, gardens and other attractions set in an oasis of natural calm.

Montjuïc, 213m (700ft) high, south of the city is the dominant feature of its skyline. Its history has been linked to the city's history since prehistoric times. The Romans later called it "Jove's Mountain" but its present name is believed to be derived from "Mountain of the Jews", after an early Jewish necropolis here. The castle (under refurbishment), standing on the bluff, dates from the 16th to 18th centuries and offers breathtaking views across the city and its coastline.

Montjuïc was the venue for the International Expo in 1929. Today many of its buildings are filled with museums. The **Museu d' Arquelogia** and the **Museu Etnològic** typify the Expo's architecture, as does the Palau Nacional, home of the Museu Nacional d'Art de Catalunya (► 44–45).

Plaça d'Espanya marks the main entrance to the city's trade fair complex with Venetian towers, and an avenue leading to Plaça de la Font Màgica – 'Magic Fountain' – a spectacular sight. The road continues up past the CaixaForum modern arts centre (► 149), Pavelló Mies van der Rohe (► 151) and the Poble Espanyol (► 152) to Fundació Joan Miró (► 40–41) and L'Anella Olímpica (► 148–149), a venue for the 1992 Olympic Games.

16K Free Cafes and restaurants (€–€€)
Espanya 50, 51, PM (Parc Monjuïc bus) Montjuïc funicular from Paral.lel Metro station

Museums

Museu d'Arquelogia: 93 424 65 77. Museu Etnològic: 93 256 34 84

5 Museu Nacional d'Art de Catalunya (MNAC)

www.mnac.es

Dominating the northern flank of Montjuïc, this imposing neoclassical palace contains a treasure trove of Catalan art spanning several centuries.

The National Museum of Catalan Art is one of the best museums of medieval and Catalan art in the world. Housed in the extravagant National Exhibition building, built as the symbol of the 1929 World Exhibition (➤ 152), the museum boasts the world's most eminent Romanesque art collection. This includes stone sculptures, wood carvings, gold and silverwork, altar cloths, enamels and coins and a beautifully presented series of 11th- and 12th-century murals, carefully stripped from church walls throughout Catalonia and precisely reconstructed in apses, as if they were still in their original locations.

The idea for this collection originated in the early 20th century when the theft of national architectural treasures in Catalonia was at its height, instigating a church-led crusade to move some of the region's most precious treasures to a safe location.

The museum's Gothic collection forms a striking contrast with more than 400 highly ornate retables and sculptures, including an extraordinary 15th-century Virgin in full flamenco dress. A somewhat fragmented collection of Renaissance and baroque paintings embraces works by Tintoretto, El Greco and Zurbarán.

The modern art collection is devoted to Catalan art from the mid-19th century to around 1930. The collection starts with works by Maria Fortuny, the earliest of the *Modernistas* and the first Catalan artist to be known widely abroad, and friends Ramon Casas, whose work once hung on the walls of Els Quatre Gats (► 105), and Santiago Rusinyol. However, the highlight is the decorative arts collection: jewellery, textiles, stained glass and ironwork.

The building also contains the Museum of Drawings and Prints, the Numismatic Museum of Catalonia, and the General Library of Art History.

15J Palau Nacional, Parc de Montjuïc 93 622 03 76 Tue–Sat 10–7, Sun and public hols 10–2:30 Moderate; free 1st Sun of month Cafe (€€) Espanya 13, 37, 50, 55, 57, PM (Parc Monjuïc bus), all buses to Plaça Espanya

6 Museu Picasso

www.museupicasso.bcn.es

This fascinating museum traces the career of the most acclaimed artist of modern times, from his early childhood sketches to the major works of later years.

The Picasso Museum contains one of the world's most important collections of Picasso's work and the only one of significance in his native country. It is housed in five medieval mansions along a cobbled lane, once one of the most desirable addresses in 13th- and 14th-century Barcelona.

Pablo Ruiz Picasso was born in Andalucía, but moved to Barcelona in 1895, aged 14. He was an exceptionally gifted artist and, by his first exhibition in 1900, was well known. In 1904 he moved to Paris, but remained in contact with Barcelona.

The museum contains work from his early years, notably a series of impressionistic landscapes and seascapes, a portrait of his aunt, Tía Pepa (1896), sketches and paintings of street scenes, *Sortida del Teatre* (1896) and La *Barceloneta* (1897), and the menu for *Els Quatre Gats* (Four Cats) cafe (➤ 105). Other works are from the Blue Period (1901–04), the Pink Period (1904–06), the Cubist (1907–20) and Neoclassical (1920–25) periods,

through to the mature works of later years. The highlight of the collection is "Las Meninas" – a series of paintings inspired by the court painting of Velázquez. There are 41 ceramic pieces donated in 1982 by his wife, Jacqueline, which demonstrate Picasso's astonishing artistic development.

21K Carrer Montcada 15–23 93 319 63 10 Tue–Sun 10–8 Moderate; free 1st Sun of month and every Sun after 3pm Cafe-restaurant (€€) Jaume I 14, 17, 19, 40, 45

7 Park Güell

Deemed a failure in its day, Gaudí's eccentric hilltop park is now considered one of the city's treasures and a unique piece of landscape design.

The architectural work of Gaudí is inseparable from Barcelona, largely thanks to his relationship with the Güells, a family of industrialists who commissioned from him a number of works. For Park Güell, Don Eusebi Güell, Gaudí's main patron,

had grand ideas for a residential English-style garden city, with 60 houses set in formal gardens. Gaudí worked on the project from 1900 to 1914, but it proved an economic disaster: only three houses were completed, and the park became city property in 1923.

The park's main entrance is marked by two eccentric pavilions. A grand stairway, ornamented by a dragon fountain, leads to a massive cavernous space, originally intended as the marketplace. Its forest of pillars supports a rooftop plaza bordered by a row of curved benches, covered in multicoloured *trencadís* (broken ceramics).

Throughout the 20ha (50 acres) of Mediterranean parkland, there are sculptures, steps and paths raised on columns of "dripping" stonework. Gaudí himself lived in one of the houses from 1906 to 1926. Built by his pupil Berenguer, it is now the Casa-Museu Gaudí and contains models, furniture, drawings and other memorabilia of the architect and his colleagues.

10C Main entrance: Carrer Olot 93 213 04 88
Daily 10–dusk Free Self-service bar
Lesseps or Vallcarca (and uphill walk with escalators)
24, 92

8 Las Ramblas

Sooner or later, every visitor joins the locals swarming day and night down Las Ramblas, one of the most famous walkways in Spain.

The name Las Ramblas, derived from *ramla* (Arabic for "torrent"), serves as a reminder that in earlier times, the street was a sandy gully that ran parallel to the medieval wall, and carried rainwater down to the sea. Today's magnificent 18th-century tree-lined walkway, running through the heart of the old city down to the port, is the pride of Barcelona. The central promenade is split into various distinctive sections strung head-to-tail, each with their own history and characteristics, from the flower stalls along Rambla de les Flors to the birdcages of Rambla dels Ocells. And it is said if you drink from the famous fountain in La Rambla de Canaletes you are sure to return to the city. The other parts of Las Ramblas are La Rambla dels Estudis, named after the university that was once here, La Rambla dels Caputxins, the section that's home to the

famous Liceu theatre, and La Rambla de Santa Mònica, the stretch nearest to the port.

Promenading Las Ramblas is never the same twice, changing with the seasons, by the day and by the hour. It's an experience eagerly shared by people from every walk of life – tourists, locals, bankers, Barça football fans, artists, beggars, street-performers, newspaper-sellers, pickpockets, nightclubbers, students, prostitutes and theatre crowds – all blending together with the noise of the traffic, the birdsong, the buskers (street musicians) and the scent of the flowers. Such is the significance to the city of this promenade *par excellence*, that two words – *ramblejar* (a verb meaning "to walk down the Rambla") and *ramblista* (an adjective describing someone addicted to the act of *ramblejar)* – have been adopted in its honour.

19K or *1d* Plenty (€–€€€) Catalunya, Drassanes, Liceu 14, 38, 59, 91 Beware of pickpockets that may be in the area

9 La Sagrada Família

www.sagradafamilia.org

Big Ben, the Eiffel Tower...most cities have a distinctive monument. Barcelona has Gaudí's Sagrada Família, his, as yet unfinished, cathedral.

Antoni Gaudí, the internationally prestigious figure of Catalan architecture, started work on La Sagrada Família (Temple of the Holy Family) in 1882, and for the latter part of his life dedicated himself entirely to his great vision for Europe's biggest cathedral.

His dream was to include three facades representing the birth, death and resurrection of Christ, and 18 mosaic-clad towers symbolizing the Twelve Apostles, the four Evangelists, the Virgin Mary and Christ. On his untimely death in 1926 (he was run over by a tram on the Gran Via), only the crypt, one of the towers, the majority of the east (Nativity) facade and the apse were completed. Ever since, the fate of the building has been the subject of often bitter debate.

With a further estimated 20 years of work (which would include the destruction of several buildings in Carrer Mallorca and Carrer Valencia), it seems that Gaudí's vision will eventually be realized. But even as it stands today, the cathedral is a world-wide symbol of Barcelona, one of the great architectural wonders of the world, and a must on every visitor's itinerary. The opportunity to watch a video about the history and construction of La Sagrada Família is included in the admission price.

23G Plaça Sagrada Família 93 208 04 14 Apr–Sep daily 9–8; Oct–Mar 9–6 Expensive; additional charge for lift Sagrada Família 19, 33, 34, 43, 44, 50, 51 Crypt museum, gift shop, lift and stairway to the towers

10 Santa Maria del Mar

This beautiful Gothic triumph was built to demonstrate Catalan supremacy in Mediterranean commerce.

The 14th-century church of Santa Maria del Mar (St Mary of the Sea) is at the heart of La Ribera (The Waterfront), the medieval city's maritime and trading district. This neighbourhood's link with the sea dates back to the 10th century, when a settlement grew up here along the seashore outside the city walls, around a chapel called Santa Maria de les Arenes (St Mary of the Sands). During the 13th century, the settlement grew and became known as Vilanova de Mar. Its identity was eventually firmly established with the transformation of the tiny chapel into the magnificent church of Santa Maria del Mar, built on what was then the seashore, as a show of maritime wealth and power. Indeed, the foundation stone commemorated the Catalan conquest of Sardinia.

The church was built between 1329 and 1384 and has a purity of style that makes it one of the finest examples of Barcelona's Gothic heritage. The plain exterior is characterized by predominantly horizontal lines and two octagonal, flat-roofed towers. Inside, the wide, soaring nave and high, narrow aisles, all supported by slim, octagonal columns, provide a great sense of spaciousness. Sadly, the ornaments of the side chapels were lost when the city was besieged, once by Bourbon troops in 1714 and again during the Spanish Civil War. The resulting bareness of the interior, apart from the sculpture of a 15th-century ship that sits atop the altar, enables you to admire the church's striking simplicity without distraction.

21K Plaça de Santa Maria
93 310 23 90 Mon–Sat 9–1:30, 4:30–8:30, Sun 10–1:30, 4:30–8:45 Free
Barceloneta, Jaume I 14, 17, 19, 36, 39, 40, 45

Best things to do

Great cafes	58–59
Top tapas bars	60–61
Excellent restaurants	62–63
Stunning views	64–65
Markets	66–67
Places to take the children	68–69
Activities	70–71
A walk through the Barri Gòtic	72–73
Parks and gardens	74–75
Modernista and modern architecture	76–77
Street art	78–79
Best shopping	80–81

Great cafes

Cacao Sampaka
At the rear of a stylish chocolate "boutique", this cafe serves hot chocolate on tap, as well as all sorts of cakes and pastries.
✉ Carrer Consell de Cent 292 ☎ 93 272 08 33 🚇 Passeig de Gràcia

Café de l'Òpera
This original 19th-century cafe is one of Barcelona's favourites, and the best terrace-cafe along the Ramblas.
✉ La Rambla 74 ☎ 93 317 75 85 🚇 Liceu

Café Zurich
Popular bar and meeting place at the top of Las Ramblas. A great place for people-watching and soaking up the atmosphere.
✉ Plaça Catalunya 1 ☎ 93 317 91 53 🚇 Catalunya

DHUB Cafe
Delicious light snacks in the courtyard of the medieval palace which houses the Disseny Hub (► 116).
✉ Carrer Montcada 12 ☎ 93 268 25 98 ⏰ Closed Mon 🚇 Jaume I
? No need to pay museum entrance

Dulcinea
The most famous chocolate shop in town. Try *melindros* (sugar-topped sponge fingers) dipped in very thick hot chocolate.
✉ Carrer Petritxol 2 ☎ 93 302 68 24 🚇 Liceu

Granja M Viader
Atmospheric old *granja* tucked down a narrow pedestrian backstreet; you can expect to queue. Try a cup of hot chocolate and one of their delicious flaky pastries.
✉ Carrer Xuclà 4 ☎ 93 318 34 86 🕒 Closed Sun 🚇 Liceu

Laie Libreria Café
This quiet, elegant cafe is located on the first floor of one of the city's better bookshops. It's great for a light lunch or coffee with a selection from their famous cake trolley.
✉ Carrer Pau Claris 85 ☎ 93 302 73 10 🚇 Passeig de Gràcia

Laie Museu Picasso
Located inside the Picasso Museum (► 46–47) but open to all, this bright cafe serves light snacks and lunches surrounded by the Gothic walls of the museum or outside in an interior courtyard.
✉ Carrer Montcada 15–23 ☎ 93 310 31 38 🚇 Jaume I ❓ No need to pay museum entrance

Pasteleria Mauri
Elegant, timeless pastry shop and cafe where high tea and coffee are served. A favourite with local residents and businesspeople.
✉ Rambla Catalunya 102 ☎ 93 215 10 20 🕒 Daily 🚇 Diagonal

Santa Marta
On the beachfront, this bohemian cafe is great for lazing on the terrace, enjoying a coffee or a drink later in the evening. On Sunday evenings there is live acoustic music and during the day free WiFi.
✉ Grau i Torres 59 ☎ 69 223 68 01 🕒 Daily 🚇 Barceloneta

Top tapas bars

Bar Pinotxo
Located to the right of the main entrance of La Boqueria, this is the best of the market's many tapas bars. It's not cheap, but a lunch of cava and fresh *chiperones* (baby octopus) is memorable.
✉ Stall 466, La Boqueria, Las Ramlas 89 ☎ 93 317 17 31
⏰ Mon–Sat 6–4:30 🚇 Liceu

Cal Pep
The queues start forming at 8pm at this hole-in-the-wall joint, testament to the fact that Cal Pep's seafood tapas is simply the best in the city.
✉ Plaça de les Olles 8 ☎ 93 310 79 61 ⏰ Closed Sun
🚇 Barceloneta

Cerveceria Catalana
This buzzing tapas bar is one the best, with mountains of fresh morsels and sizzling seafood. Take a seat at the bar if there's room – it's more fun!
✉ Carrer Mallorca 236 ☎ 93 216 03 68 🚇 Passeig de Gràcia

Euskal Etxea
Of the many bars in Barcelona selling *pintxos* (Basque-style tapas) this is one of the best. Get here are at 7pm as they sell out fast.
✉ Placeta Montcada 1–3 ☎ 93 310 21 85 ⏰ Closed Sun
🚇 Jaume I

La Plata
One of several *tascas* (traditional bars) on this narrow medieval street, specializing in whitebait and tomato and onion salads.
✉ Carrer Mercè 28 ☎ 93 315 10 09 ⏰ Closed Sun
🚇 Barceloneta

Quimet i Quimet
Cramped neighbourhood *bodega* serving excellent tapas – both traditional and creative – and wine by the glass.
✉ Carrer de Poeta Cabanyes 25 ☎ 93 442 31 42
⏲ Mon–Fri noon–4pm, 7–10:30pm, Sat noon–4pm
🚇 Paral.lel

Taller de Tapas
Written menus and helpful staff take the headache out of tapas ordering. The quality is excellent and there branches across town.
✉ Carrer Argenteria 51 ☎ 93 268 85 59 🚇 Jaume 1
✉ Plaça Sant Josep Oriol 9 ☎ 93 301 80 20 🚇 Liceu

Tapaç 24
Mouth-watering traditional tapas and seafood are served alongside signature ham and cheese toasties. Friendly, helpful service.
✉ Carrer de Diputació 269 ☎ 93 488 09 77; www.carlesabellan.com ⏲ Closed Sun 🚇 Passeig de Gràcia

Vaso de Oro
Try the melt-in-your-mouth *solomillo,* beer made on the premises and superb tapas in what must be the narrowest bar in Barcelona.
✉ Carrer Balboa 6 ☎ 93 319 30 98 🚇 Barceloneta

El Xampanyet
Always packed, this tile-lined cava bar is an institution. Anchovies, the house speciality, are displayed on the marble counter.
✉ Montcada 22 ☎ 93 319 70 03 ⏲ Closed Sun eve, Mon
🚇 Jaume I

Excellent restaurants

Alkimia (€€€)
Superb restaurant with chef Jordi Vila at the helm, serving wonderfully innovative dishes in a sleek dining room.
✉ Carrer Industria 79 ☎ 93 207 61 15 ⏲ Lunch, dinner. Closed Sat and Sun
🚇 Sagrada Família

Can Majó (€€)
The city's top seafood restaurant. The *suquet de peix* (mixed fish casserole), *arroz negre* (black rice) with *bacalao* (salt cod) or lobster, and *centollos* (crabs from the north coast) are delicious.
✉ Carrer Almirall Aixada 23 ☎ 93 221 54 55 ⏲ Closed Sun dinner and Mon
🚇 Barceloneta

Casa Calvet (€€€)
Gaudí's first apartment building in Barcelona is now a sumptuous restaurant offering sophisticated French and Catalan cuisine.
✉ Carrer Casp 48 ☎ 93 412 40 12 ⏲ Closed Sun 🚇 Urquinaona

Cinc Sentits (€€€)
A minimalist restaurant serving New Catalan Cuisine. Try the tasting menu with wine pairing for the full experience.
✉ Carrer Aribau 58 ☎ 93 323 94 91 ⏲ Closed Mon dinner and Sun
🚇 Passeig de Gràcia

Els Fogons de la Barceloneta (€€)
This informal restaurant on the main square in Barceloneta offers delicious plates of tapas and rice dishes at accessible prices.
✉ Plaça de la Font, Mercado de la Barceloneta ☎ 93 224 26 26; www.elsfogonsdelabarceloneta.com ⏲ Closed Sun eve and Mon 🚇 Barceloneta

El Lobito (€€€)
There is no menu: just take a seat and mountains of the freshest seafood in all its forms will be brought to your table.
✉ Carrer Ginebra 9 ☎ 93 319 91 64 ⏲ Closed Sun and Mon 🚇 Barceloneta

Moments (€€€)
To really spoil yourself, experience the beautifully judged, Catalan-inspired cooking in the city's latest top luxury hotel.
✉ Mandarin Oriental, Passeig de Gràcia 38–40 ☎ 93 151 87 83; www.mandarinoriental.com ⏲ Closed Sun eve and Mon 🚇 Passeig de Gràcia

Set Portes (€€)
One of Barcelona's most historic restaurants, serving excellent Catalan cuisine in traditional surroundings.
✉ Passeig de Isabel II 14 ☎ 93 319 30 33 ⏲ Lunch, dinner 🚇 Barceloneta

Tapioles 53 (€€)
This intimate space serves European and Asian dishes. Ingredients are sourced daily from local markets. Reservations are essential.
✉ Carrer Tapioles 53 ☎ 93 329 22 38 ⏲ Dinner only; closed Sun and Mon 🚇 Paral.lel

Torre de Alta Mar (€€€)
Classy cuisine served in a glass-enclosed dining room perched on top of a cable-car tower. Needless to say, the views are fabulous.
✉ Passeig de Joan de Borbó 88 ☎ 93 221 00 07 ⏲ Lunch, dinner. Closed Sun 🚇 Barceloneta

Stunning views

Casa Milà (La Pedrera) rooftop terrace (➤ 36–37)

Mirablau (➤ 161)

Mirador de l'Alcalde (➤ 153)

Monument a Colom (➤ 91)

Museu Nacional d'Art de Catalunya (MNAC) terrace (➤ 44–45)

Park Güell (► 48–49)

La Sagrada Família (► 52–53)

Telèferic de Montjuïc (► 68)

Torre de Collserola (► 159)

Torre de Alta Mar (► 63)

Markets

Barceloneta

This imaginative makeover of a 19th-century market is a landmark. Excellent bars and restaurants jostle with traditional fish stalls.

✉ Plaça Font 1 ⏰ Mon, Sat 7–3, Tue–Thu 7–3, 5–8:30 🚇 Barceloneta

La Boqueria

Superb 19th-century market hall at the heart of Las Ramblas. Top-quality fresh produce including fish, fruit, vegetables and herbs.

⏰ Mon–Sat 8–8 🚇 Liceu

La Concepció

In the heart of the Eixample, this *Modernista* neighbourhood food market displays a feast of fresh produce under an impressive iron structure.

✉ Carrer Aragó 311 ⏰ Mon 8–15, Tue–Fri 8–8, Sat 8–4 🚇 Passeig de Gràcia/Girona

Fira de Santa Lucia
Located in front of the cathedral (➤ 38) the Christmas market is the biggest event during *Nadal*. Christmas trees and decorations, Nativity figures, plus artisan crafts and gifts in hundreds of stalls.
✉ Plaça de la Seu 🕐 End Nov–23 Dec 10–8 🚇 Jaume 1, Liceu

Plaça del Pi
Outdoor market selling home-made honey, herbs and cheeses.
🕐 First and third Fri, Sat and Sun of month 10–10 🚇 Liceu

Plaça Reial
Browse among the stands displaying coins and stamps every Sunday. Also stalls with general items of interest for sale.
🕐 Sun 9–2:30 🚇 Liceu, Drassanes

Plaça Sant Josep Oriol
Art market in one of the Barri Gòtic's picturesque squares.
🕐 Sat 11–10, Sun 10–3 🚇 Liceu

Raval craft and hippy market
Funky, handmade clothes, crafts and accessories, plus Moroccan tea stalls make up this small but eclectic market.
✉ Rambla del Raval (northern end) 🕐 Weekends only
🚇 Sant Antoni, Liceu

Santa Caterina
A modern, new market, held in the Barri Gòtic, with striking architecture (including 109 arches) featuring a variety of traditional stalls, restaurants and bars.
✉ Francesc Cambó 16 🕐 Thu, Fri 7:30am–8:30pm, Tue, Wed, Sat 7:30–3:30, Mon 7:30–2 🚇 Jaume I

Places to take the children

L'Aquàrium

Aquatic life on display and a tunnel through the shark tank.
Moll d'Espanya, Port Vell 93 221 74 74; www.aquariumbcn.com
Jul–Aug daily 9:30am–11pm; Sep–Jun 9:30–9:30 Expensive
Barceloneta, Drassanes

Beaches

The city has 4km (2.5 miles) of clean, sandy beaches with playgrounds, palm-lined promenades and shower facilities.
Platja de Barceloneta, Nova Icària, Bogatell and La Nova Mar Bella
Ciutadella, Selva de Mar, Poble Nou, Barceloneta

Cable car and gondolier ride

Take a ride in a cable car over the marina up to Montjuïc followed by a journey to the summit in a state-of-the-art glass gondola.
Transbordador Aeri Torre de Sant Sebastià, Barceloneta 93 225 27 18 Daily 10:30–8 (dusk Oct–May) Moderate Barceloneta 17, 39
Telefèric de Montjuïc Avinguda de Miramar 933 289 003; www.tmb.cat Jun–Sep daily 10am–9pm; Apr, May, Oct 10–7; Nov–Mar daily 10–6 Moderate Funicular de Montjuïc 50, 55

CaixaForum

This dynamic arts centre (➤ 149) is a good midday-heat or wet-weather option. Drawing packs for children and weekend activities.
Avenue Marquès de Comillas 6–8 93 476 86 00 Sun–Fri 10am–8pm, Sat 10–10 Free Espanya 50, 55, 61

Camp Nou and Museu del Futbol Club Barcelona

A must for all children who are keen on football (➤ 156).
Camp Nou – Gate 7 or 9 (Carrer Arístides Maillol) 93 496 36 00; www.fcbarcelona.com Mon–Sat 10–8, Sun 10–2 Moderate Cafe

Montjuïc

Beyond the castle are child-friendly museums and sports facilities,

and a landscaped park dotted with playgrounds (► 42–43).
Free Cafes and restaurants (€–€€) Espanya 50, 51, PM (Parc Monjuïc bus) Montjuïc funicular from Paral.lel Metro station

Museu de la Cera

Atmospheric old waxwork museum with a collection ranging from Catalan dignitaries to Indiana Jones and Don Quijote, with the obligatory Chamber-of-Horrors finale.
Passeig de la Banca 7 93 317 26 49 Jul–Sep daily 10–10; Oct–Jun Mon–Fri 10–1:30, 4–7:30, Sat–Sun 11–2, 4:30–8:30 Moderate
Drassanes

Parc d'Atraccions del Tibidabo

An authentic, old-fashioned fairground atmosphere with carousels, bumper cars, a hall of mirrors and an open ferris wheel.
Plaça Tibidabo 3–4 93 211 79 42 Jul–Aug Wed–Sat noon–11; call ahead for other times Expensive FGC Tibidabo, then Tramvia Blau, then Funicular del Tibidabo

Parc Zoològic

Spain's top zoo has a section for the under-fives, where children can stroke farm animals, and a dolphinarium with regular shows.
Parc de la Ciutadella 93 225 67 80; www.zoobarcelona.com
Jun–Sep 10–7; Mar–May, Oct 10–6; Nov–Feb 10–5 Expensive
Barceloneta

Poble Espanyol

This "model village" contains examples of Spain's regional architecture, from Castilian castles to pretty whitewashed houses.
Avinguda Marqués de Comillas s/n 93 508 63 00 Mon 9am–8pm, Tue–Thu 9am–2am, Fri 9am–4am, Sat 9am–5am, Sun 9am–midnight
Moderate Espanya

Activities

Walking: Take a stroll down Las Ramblas (► 50–51), the vibrant heart of the city and then around the marina to the Passeig Marítim and along the beaches (► 114–115).

Rickshaws: These three-wheeled trixi taxis are a fun way to get around. Hail them on the street around the old city and Port Vell.
✉ Avingunda de la Catedral ⏲ Daily 11–8 ☎ www.trixi.com

Bus tours: A circuit around the city on the Bus Turístic with 25 stops at key points of interest is a good way to see the sights.
✉ Plaça de Catalunya (or any of its 25 stops) ⏲ First bus leaves Plaça de Catalunya at 9am 🚇 Catalunya

Cycling: This has taken off in a big way in Barcelona, prompted by better cycle lanes and Bicing, the city's bike-share service (for residents only). Inexpensive bicycle hire for tourists is available at the tourist office and outlets throughout the city. Many companies offer guided tours.

Fat Tyre Bike Tours

✉ Escudellers 48 ☎ 93 301 36 12; www.fattirebiketoursbarcelona.com

Moderate

Budget Bikes

✉ Carrer d'Estruc ☎ 38 93 304 18 85 Catalunya

***Golondrinas* (pleasure boats):** Take a pleasure boat tour of the old harbour (➤ 100) or along the coast to Port Fòrum.

✉ Moll de les Drassanes Plaça Portal de la Pau ☎ 93 442 31 06

Jogging and running: Start at Barceloneta beach and continue to the Hotel Arts (about 2km/1.25 miles) or on to the Forum complex in Poble Nou (about 5km/3 miles). Montjuïc is also a popular option and offers more shade.

Barceloneta, Ciutadella-Vila Olímpica, El Maresme-Forúm

Swimming: Piscines Bernat Picornell. This attractive swimming pool in Montjuïc is part of the Anella Olímpica, or Olympic complex.

✉ Avinguda de l'Estadi ☎ 93 423 40 41 Paral.lel, then funicular to Montjuïc 55

Watersports: On Mar Bella beach there's a friendly sailing school that also rents outs catamarans, canoes and windsurfers by the hour. Barceloneta Beach is the best for low-key body surfing but there's no board hire available.

✉ Mar Bella Beach ☎ 93 221 04 32; www.basenautica.org

Ciutadella-Villa Olímpica

a walk through the Barri Gòtic

Leave tiny Plaça Nova on the right-hand side of the cathedral via the Portal del Bisbe (part of the Roman wall) into Carrer del Bisbe. Turn first left into Carrer de Santa Llúcia.

Note the tiny chapel of Santa Llúcia to your right, and the Gothic Archdeacon's House (Casa de l'Ardiaca) to your left. Just beyond is the main entrance to the Catedral (➤ 38–39).

From Plaça de la Seu, follow Carrer dels Comtes to the left of the cathedral, past Museu Frederic Marès (➤ 93). Turn left into Baixada de Santa Clara to Plaça del Rei (➤ 97). Return to the cathedral and skirt round its buttresses past the 14th-century Canon's House (Casa del Cánonges).

Stone plaques on the facade portray towers supported by winged goats with lions' feet, heraldic symbols of medieval Barcelona.

Turn sharp left, then left again onto Carrer del Bisbe, go under a bridge and into Plaça Sant Jaume (► 99). Take Carrer de la Ciutat, then first left to Plaça Sant Just.

Església dels Sants Just i Pastor is reputedly Barcelona's oldest church.

Leave the square along Carrer del Lledó. Turn right and walk to tiny Plaça Traginer and the most intact part of the old Roman walls.

Constructed between AD270 and 310, Barcelona's Roman walls were outgrown by the 11th century.

For more Roman vestiges, turn right into Carrer Correu Vell and right again into Carrer Regomir.

At No 3 is Pati Llimona, where the remains of a Roman dwelling are visible through a glass floor.

Continue walking along Carrer Regomir to Plaça Nova.

Distance 2km (1.25 miles)
Time 1 hour (excluding visits)
Start/end point Plaça Nova ✚ *3b*
Ⓜ Catalunya, Urquinaona
Coffee break Bliss (€), Plaça de Sant Just 4, 93 268 10 22

Parks and gardens

Jardí Botànic

A contemporary landscape garden divided into eight different zones displaying plants from Australia to the Balearic Islands.

www.jardibotanic.bcn.es

15J Carrer Doctor Fonti Quer 2 93 424 50 52 Jun–Aug daily 10–8; Apr, May, Sep daily 10–7; Feb, Mar, Oct 10–6; Nov–Jan 10–5 Inexpensive Snack bar 50, 55, PM (Parc Montjuïc) bus

Montjuïc

The city's finest and largest park, rising over the harbour, offers viewpoints, exotic gardens and fine museums (► 42–43).

16K Snack bars and restaurants Espanya 50, 55, PM (Parc Montjuïc) bus Montjuïc funicular from Paral.lel

Palau Reial de Pedralbes gardens

The landscaped park surrounding the Royal Palace of Pedralbes is perfect for a picnic (► 158–159).

2C Avinguda de la Diagonal 686 Park: daily 10–dusk Park: free Palau Reial 7, 33, 67, 68, 74, 75

Parc de la Ciutadella

A great place for a walk, a picnic or boating on the lake (► 120).

22K Main entrance: Passeig Picasso Daily 10–dusk Snack bars Arc de Triomf, Barceloneta, Jaume I

Parc de la Creueta del Coll

An old stone quarry makes for Barcelona's most unusual park, with an enormous bronze sculpture by Chillida.

10B Carrer Cardedeu s/n 10–dusk Snack bar 27, 28, 92

Parc de l'Espanya Industrial

Located on the site of an old textile factory, the park has some surreal sculptures and a small boating lake (► 150).

15G Carrer de Muntadas Snack bar Sants-Estació

Parc de l'Estació del Nord

Behind the main bus station this modern park borders on land art, with evocative sculptures by US artist Beverly Pepper.

22J Carrer Napoles 1 Open all the time Arc de Triomf

Parc de Joan Miró (Parc de l'Escoraxdor)

A popular park with pergolas and shady palm trees. Its most famous feature is the sculpture *Dona i Ocell* (Woman and Bird) by Miró (► 150–151).

16G Carrer de Tarragona Snack bar Tarragona, Espanya

Parc del Laberint

An extensive garden with fountains, sculptures and a beautiful maze at its heart, from which the park takes its name. Situated on the wooded slopes of Vall d'Hebron.

10A (off map) Passeig dels Castanyers 1–17, Vall d'Hebron 93 428 25 00 Daily 10–dusk, ticket office closes one hour before closing time Inexpensive; free Wed and Sun Snack bar Mundet 10, 27, 60, 73, 76

Park Güell

Gaudí's fairy-tale park overlooking the city (► 48–49).

10C Main entrance: Carrer Olot 93 219 38 11 Daily 10–dusk Free Snack bar Lesseps or Vallcarca (steep uphill walk) 24, 28

Modernista and modern architecture

Casa Batlló (► 134–135)

Casa Milà (La Pedrera) (► 36–37)

Casa Lleó-Morera (► 135)

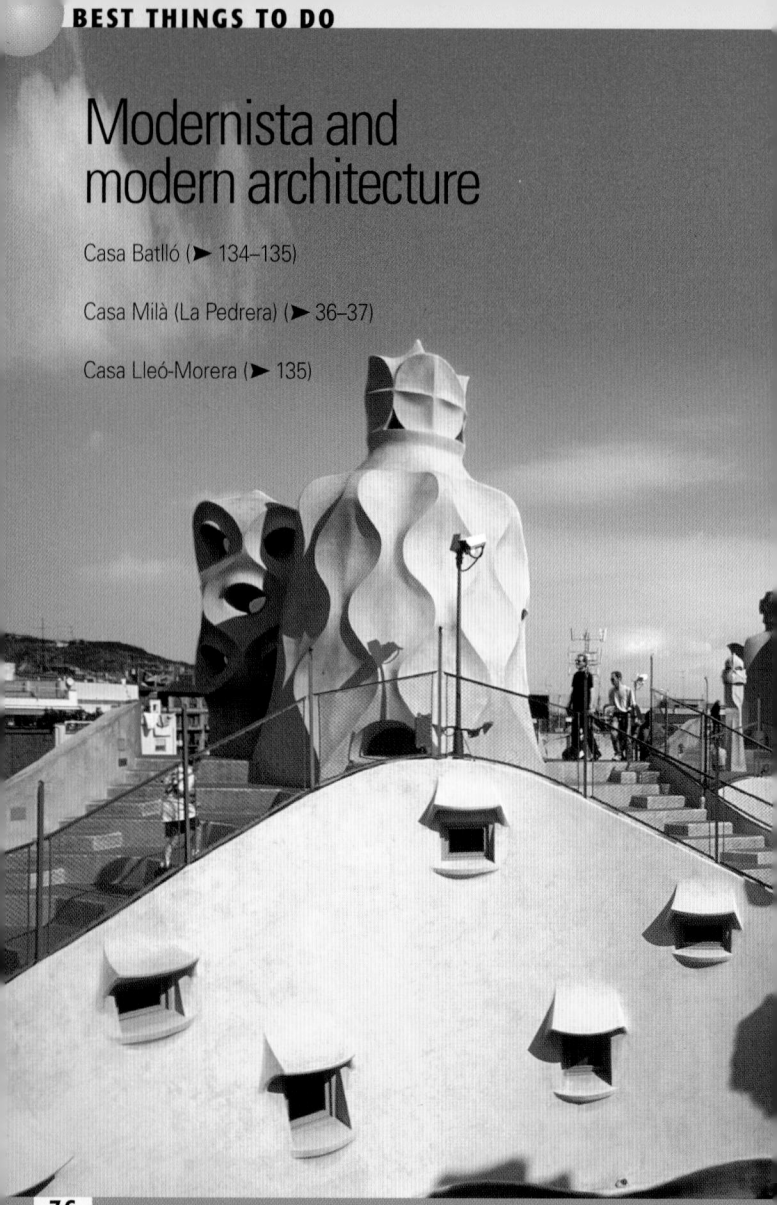

Fundació Antoni Tàpies (► 130)

Fundació Joan Miró (► 40–41)

Hospital de la Santa Creu i Sant Pau (► 132–133)

Palau Güell (► 95)

Palau de la Música Catalana (► 118–119)

Pavelló Mies van der Rohe (► 151)

La Sagrada Família (► 52–53)

Street art

Peix (Fish)
Designed by American architect Frank Gehry, the giant bronze fish by the beach is the city's maritime symbol.
✉ Hotel Arts, Passeig Marítim, Port Olímpica

Cap de Barcelona (Barcelona Head)
A giant mosaic sculpture (below) by Roy Lichtenstein at the eastern end of the waterfront promenade by the main post office.
✉ Plaça Antonio López

Gambrinus
A giant rooftop fibreglass lobster by Xavier Mariscal.
✉ Moll de la Fusta, Passeig de Colom

Dona i Ocell (Woman and Bird)
A startling sculpture (right) covered in multicoloured ceramic fragments, in Parc de Joan Miró (➤ 150–151).
✉ Carrer de Tarragona

Nüvol i Cadira (Cloud and Chair)
An eye-catching tangle of wire and tubes on the roof of Fundació Antoni Tàpies (➤ 130).
✉ Carrer d'Aragó 255

El Gato (The Cat)
This voluptous bronze cat figure is by Columbian artist Fernando Botero.
✉ Rambla del Raval

Estil Ferit (Homage to Barceloneta)
German artist Rebecca Horn's stacked steel cubes are homage to the old *chiringuitos* (beach bars) of Barceloneta beach.
✉ Platja de la Barceloneta

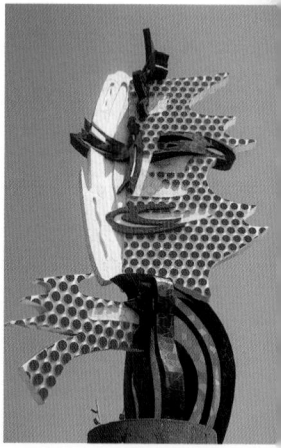

Els Gegants, La Senyera i Les Nens
This mural on the wall of the city's architecture school was designed by Picasso and features Catalan folkloric figures.
✉ Plaça Nova 1

La Senyoreta del Paraigua (The Lady with the Umbrella)
This elegant belle époque sculpture is the work of Josep Foresteré, designer of the park where it is located.
✉ Parc de la Ciutadella (inside zoo)

Barcino
Outside the main cathedral, Joan Brossa's giant bronze letters are homage to the old Roman city.
✉ Plaça de la Seu

Best shopping

Art Escudellers
Huge emporium selling Spanish pottery and ceramics, from factory pieces to arty individual designs. In the basement are a wine cellar, delicatessen and wine bar where you can sample the local products.
✉ Carrer Escudellers 23 ☎ 93 412 68 01 🚇 Liceu, Drassanes

Caleum
For a great gift to take home, this lovely shop sells cakes, jams, honey and other delights produced in convents and monasteries all over Spain. There is a cafe on site to try before you buy.
✉ Carrer Palla 8 ☎ 93 302 69 93 🚇 Liceu

Custo Barcelona
Another successful export, Custo's loud and funky T-shirts have now reached celebrity status. They have recently added eclectic coats and skirts to their range.
✉ Plaça de les Olles 7 (also Las Ramblas 109) ☎ 93 268 78 93; www.custo-barcelona.com 🚇 Jaume I

Loewe
One of the most celebrated leather-goods companies in the world, located in Domènech i Montaner's *Modernista* Lleó-Morera building.
✉ Passeig de Gràcia 35 ☎ 93 216 04 00 🚇 Passeig de Gràcia

La Manual Alpargatera
This shop has been making traditional Spanish espadrilles, with esparto soles, by hand since 1910. Their footwear has been worn by celebrities including Michael Douglas and Jack Nicholson.
✉ Carrer Avinyó 7 ☎ 93 301 01 72 🚇 Jaume I, Liceu

Markets
Food shopping doesn't get much better than at the neighbourhood markets. Colourful stalls groaning with fresh fruit, olives, hams and cheeses are perfect for putting together a delicious picnic (► 66–67).

Museum and gallery shops
Almost without exception, Barcelona's museum and gallery shops offer a high-quality and imaginative mix of gifts, publications, art reproductions plus educational and fun stuff for kids.

Vinçon
This design 'department store' is Barcelona's answer to the British designer Terance Conran. Trendy yet practical household articles at accessible prices.
✉ Passeig de Gràcia 96 ☎ 93 215 60 50 🚇 Passeig de Gràcia

Xocoa
The offspring of this dynasty of chocolate-makers has created a brilliant concept of designer-packaged chocolate bars and bon-bons in unusual flavours.
✉ Carrer Petrixol 11–13 (and all over the city) ☎ 93 301 11 97; www.xocoa-bcn.com 🚇 Liceu

Zara
The Spanish fashion label that conquered the world has a bigger range at better prices on its home turf. Larger stores include Zara Home (textiles and homeware), which is exclusive to Spain.
✉ Passeig de Gràcia 16 (and all over the city) ☎ 93 318 76 75; www.zara.com 🚇 Passeig de Gràcia

Exploring

Las Ramblas and around 85–112

La Ribera to Port Olímpic 113–126

The Eixample and Gràcia 127–146

Montjuïc to Sants 147–154

Pedralbes and Tibidabo 155–161

Ever since it was founded more than 2,000 years ago, Barcelona has been striving to become a great metropolis. To its inhabitants, it is not Spain's second city but the capital of Catalonia; not a Spanish metropolis but a European one, and the Spanish leader in both *haute couture* and *haute cuisine*. The best time to see Barcelona in its true colours is after FC Barça wins an important match, and the streets erupt to the sound of car horns and popping champagne corks.

Visitors to Barcelona, on the other hand, are entranced by the Mediterranean atmosphere of the city, the richness of its art and architectural treasures both ancient and modern, the proud but not narrowly nationalistic character of the people, the strong tradition of theatre and music and the exuberant nightlife. In this dynamic and passionate city, it is easy to live life to the fullest, both day and night.

Las Ramblas and around

This historic part of town has a wide choice of hotels and restaurants, shops and markets and top bars and clubs. Las Ramblas, one long tree-lined thoroughfare divided into five distinct sections, stretches from Plaça de Catalunya, Barcelona's central square, towards the waterfront. It is the place to watch street entertainers and the ceaseless flow of pedestrians.

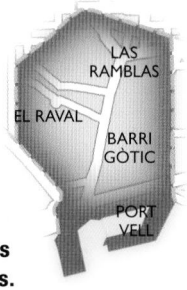

To the east of Las Ramblas is the Barri Gòtic (Gothic Quarter), a maze of narrow streets around the cathedral, medieval palaces and churches. Beyond is Port Vell (Old Port), the colourful harbourside, with a marvellous state-of-the-art aquarium, and the Maremagnum, a huge entertainment and shopping complex. Gaudí's magnificent Palau Güell, just off the Ramblas, is set in the lower side of El Raval – a run-down mix of medieval streets and gloomy alleyways. By contrast, the upper part of El Raval is dominated by the Museu d'Art Contemporàni (MACBA), the city's contemporary art museum set amid stylish restaurants and hip boutiques.

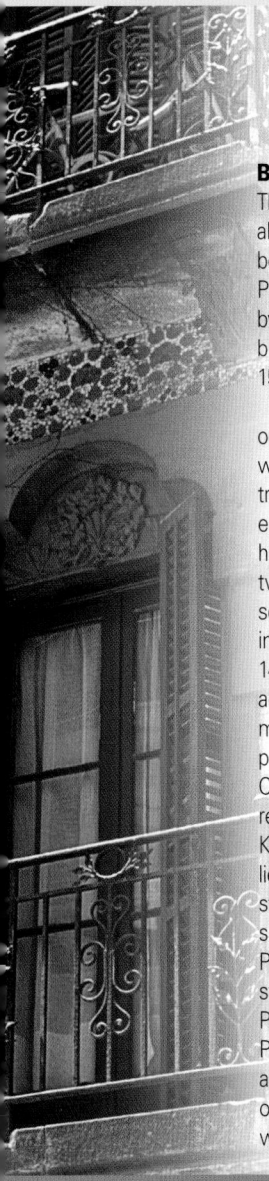

BARRI GÒTIC

The tightly packed maze of narrow streets and alleyways of Barcelona's Ciutat Vella (Old City), bordered by Las Ramblas, the Ciutadella Park, Plaça Catalunya and the sea, was once enclosed by medieval city walls and, until the massive building boom of the Eixample (► 129), 150 years ago, refocused the entire city.

At its heart is the Barri Gòtic (Gothic Quarter), one of several clearly identifiable *barris* or districts which make up the Old City. Its roots can be traced back to 15BC, when Roman soldiers established a settlement called Barcino on a slight hill here called Mons Taber. Today's cluster of dark, twisting streets, quiet patios, sun-splashed squares and grand Gothic buildings was built inside the Roman fortifications during the 13th and 14th centuries when Barcelona, along with Genoa and Venice, was one of the three most important merchant cities in the Mediterranean and possessed untold riches. Its crowning glory, the Catedral (► 38–39), is surrounded by former residences of the counts of Barcelona and the Kings of Catalonia and Aragón. To the northwest lies Carrer Portaferrissa, the principal shopping street, with high-street fashion boutiques and shopping arcades. To the south lies the spacious Plaça Sant Jaume (► 99) and a cobweb of narrow streets and interconnecting squares, including Plaça Sant Felip Neri, with its fine baroque church, Plaça del Pi, its market of local produce (► 67), and leafy Plaça Sant Josep Oriol, the 'Montmartre of Barcelona', where local artists display their works at weekends and buskers entertain the cafe

crowds. Just off the square, the narrow streets bounded by Carrer Banys Nous, Call and Bisbe once housed a rich Jewish ghetto called *El Call*, but now the area is better known for its antiques shops.

As the city grew more prosperous in the early Middle Ages, new *barris* developed around the Roman perimeter, including La Mercè to the south and La Ribera to the east. La Ribera is the old city's most fashionable district, with a plethora of cutting-edge cafes and boutiques, and dominated by the majestic Santa Maria del Mar church (► 54–55). The area south of Carrer de Ferran – La Mercè – is focused around the elegant, arcaded Plaça Reial (► 98) and the Church of La Mercè, Barcelona's patron Virgin.

✚ 20K or *3c*

CATEDRAL

Best places to see, pages 38–39.

DRASSANES REIALS AND MUSEU MARÍTIM

The Museu Marítim (Maritime Museum) is in the magnificent Drassanes Reials (Royal Shipyards), a splendid example of Gothic civil architecture. Since the 13th century, these yards have been dedicated to the construction of ships for the Crowns of Catalonia and Aragon. Part of the shipyard is closed due to refurbishment until 2013.

Today, their vast cathedral-like, stone-vaulted halls contain maps, charts, paintings, pleasure craft and a huge range of other seafaring memorabilia chronicling the remarkable maritime history of Barcelona. The most impressive exhibit is a 60m (66-yard) replica of *La Real*, flagship of Don Juan of Austria, which forms part of an exciting 45-minute spectacle – "The Great Sea Adventure". Through headphones, visual and acoustic effects, visitors can experience life as a galley slave, encounter a Caribbean storm, and explore the seabed on board *Ictineo*, claimed to be the world's first submarine and built by Catalan inventor Narcís Monturiol. A visit to the 19th-century schooner *Santa Eulàlia* moored in nearby Port Vell is included in the ticket.

www.museumaritimbarcelona.org

19L Avinguda de les Drassanes s/n 93 342 99 29 Daily 10–8

Inexpensive, free after 3pm on Sun Cafe-restaurant (€€) Drassanes

14, 18, 36, 38, 57, 59, 64, 91 Library, bookshop, gift shop

MERCAT DE LA BOQUERIA

Of more than 40 food markets in Barcelona, La Boqueria is the best and the busiest – always bustling with local shoppers, restaurateurs, gourmands and tourists. Its cavernous market hall (best entered through an imposing wrought-iron entranceway halfway up Las Ramblas) was built in the 1830s to house the food stalls that cluttered Las Ramblas and surrounding streets.

Inside is a riot of noise, aromas and colours, with a myriad of stalls offering all the specialities of the Mediterranean and the Catalonian hinterland – mouth-watering displays of fruit and vegetables, a glistening array of seafood and fish, endless strings of sausages, haunches of ham and sweetly scented bunches of herbs.

19J or *1b* Rambla 91 93 318 25 84
Mon–Sat 8–8:30; closed public hols
Bar Pinotxo, ➤ 60 Liceu

MONUMENT A COLOM

This vast monument, commemorating the return of Christopher Columbus to Barcelona in 1493 from his first trip to the Americas, stands outside the naval headquarters of Catalonia, at the seaward end of the Ramblas. It was designed by Gaietà Buigas for the Universal Exposition of 1888, with Columbus standing at the top of a column 50m (164ft) high, pointing out to sea – towards Italy! Take the lift to the top for a bird's-eye view of the harbourfront.

19L or *1f* Plaça Portal de la Pau 93 302 52 24 May–Oct daily 9–8:30; Nov–Apr 10–6:30 Inexpensive Drassanes 14, 20, 21, 36, 57, 59, 64

MUSEU D'ART CONTEMPORANI DE BARCELONA (MACBA)

The Barcelona Museum of Contemporary Art (MACBA), which celebrated its 15th anniversary in 2010, focuses on the art movements of the second half of the 20th century.The building, itself a work of art, was designed by the American architect Richard Meier. It has been the subject of much controversy but is increasingly being included as one of Barcelona's must-see landmarks. The vast white edifice with swooping ramps and glass-walled galleries almost upstages the works on display. Its location – surrounded by shabby old houses in the once rundown district of Raval – has spearheaded investment in the neighbourhood.

MACBA specializes in temporary exhibitions of contemporary art but also has an extensive collection (exhibited in rotation) which covers the 1940s to the 1990s, with special emphasis on Catalan and Spanish artists. It contains works by Klee, Miró and Tàpies, Joan Brossa, Maurizio Cattelan and Damien Hirst.

www.macba.cat
19J Plaça dels Àngels 1 93 412 08 10 Mon–Fri 11–7:30, Sat 10–8, Sun and public hols 10–3. Longer opening hours in summer. Guided tours in English: Mon 6pm (free) Moderate Cafe (€) in summer Catalunya, Universitat

MUSEU FREDERIC MARÈS

This museum was founded by local artist Frederic Marès, Spain's most prolific collector, in 1946. The entrance is via a beautiful medieval courtyard, which was once part of the Royal Palace of the Kings and Queens of Catalonia and Aragon. The museum itself is divided into three main sections: Roman artefacts in the basement, the sculpture collection on the first floor, featuring religious works from the Romanesque period to the 20th century, and the 'Sentimental Museum' on the other floors, which portrays daily life from the 15th to 20th centuries through astonishing household items. Highlights include the women's section (with collections of fans, parasols, jewellery and hat pins), the smoker's room, and the entertainments room, with its puppet theatres, wind-up toys and dolls. The museum is closed, due to reopen spring 2011.

www.museumares.bcn.cat
20K or *4c* Plaça de Sant Iu 5–6 93 256 35 00 Courtyard: Tue–Sun 10–10 Courtyard free Jaume I 17, 19, 40, 45 Museum closed until spring 2011. Courtyard with interacive panels open

MUSEU D'HISTÒRIA DE LA CIUTAT

The Museu d'Història de la Ciutat (City History Museum) is divided into several sections in various locations around the Plaça del Rei (► 97). To start, visitors can familiarize themselves with the earliest origins of the city by wandering around along the underground walkways beneath the square, which explore a vast area of excavations that have exposed evidence of the ancient Roman settlement of Barcino.

Casa Padellàs, a medieval mansion, was moved here stone by stone when the Via Laietana was created in 1930. Inside the mansion, carefully selected and thoroughly documented exhibits trace Barcelona's remarkable evolution through 2,000 years of history from its beginnings as a Roman trading post to its status as a wealthy 18th-century metropolis. The highlight is the majestic barrel-vaulted banqueting hall Soló de Tinell, the seat of the first Catalan parliament, and where Ferdinand and Isabella were said to have fêted Christopher Columbus on his return from the Americas.

www.museuhistoria.bcn.es

20K or *4c* Plaça del Rei s/n 93 256 21 00 Apr–Sep Tue–Sun 10–8; Oct–Mar Tue–Sat 10–2, 4–7, Sun 10–8 Moderate; free 1st Sat pm of month Jaume I, Liceu 17, 19, 40, 45, 59 Guided tours by appointment

PALAU GÜELL

This extraordinary building, constructed between 1886 and 1888 and declared a World Cultural Heritage site by UNESCO, was Antoni Gaudí's first major architectural project, commissioned by the Güell family.

The facade is particularly striking, with its twin arches leading into the central vestibule. Off the latter are various rooms decorated with *Modernista* fittings. A ramp leads down to the basement stables, constructed with bare-brick columns and arches. The rooftop terrace is a mixture of random spires, battlements and chimneys of differing shapes and sizes, decorated with coloured ceramic mosaics. Look closely and on one you will find a reproduction of Cobi, the 1992 Barcelona Olympics mascot. Unfortunately, the Güell family did not live here long. In 1936, the palace was confiscated by Spanish Civil War anarchists, who used it as their military headquarters and prison. Closed for renovation, it is due to reopen the end of 2011.

www.palauguell.cat

19K or *1d* Carrer Nou de la Rambla 3–5 93 317 39 74 Liceu

PLAÇA DE CATALUNYA

The Plaça de Catalunya is the heart of Barcelona and the hub of the city's transport system. It was first landscaped at the end of the 19th century and became of major importance as the pivotal point between the old and new city: the Barri Gòtic (► 86–88) to the east, the Eixample district (► 128–129) to the north and west, and, to the southeast, Las Ramblas (► 50–51) running down to the port.

Its main landmarks today are the head office of Banco Espanol de Crédito, former headquarters of the unified Socialist Party of Catalonia during the Civil War; the El Corte Inglés department store and a medley of fountains and statues, including work by important sculptors such as Gargallo, Marès and Subirachs. Today, its benches, trees and splashing fountains make it a popular place to meet.

20H Catalunya

PLAÇA DEL REI

The charming King's Square was once a bustling medieval marketplace. Today, it forms a frequent backdrop to summer open-air concerts and theatrical events, especially during the Grec festival (► 25), and is the location of the City History Museum (► 94), a huge section of which is housed in the **Palau Reial Major** (Great Royal Palace), former residence of the Counts of Barcelona.

It was on the steps leading up to the Palau Reial Major that King Ferdinand and Queen Isabella are said to have received Columbus on his return from his first voyage to America in 1493. Inside, the Spanish Inquisition once sat in the Saló del Tinell, exploiting the local myth that should any prisoner lie, the stones on the ceiling would move. Today, the hall functions as an exhibition area.

On the north side of the square is the chapel of Santa Agata (also part of the royal palace), which contains a precious 15th-century altarpiece by Jaume Huguet. On the opposite side of the square, the Palau de Lloctinent (Palace of the Deputy) was built in 1549 for the Catalan representative of the king in Madrid. A visit to the museum includes viewing an extensive swathe of the old Roman city, including mosaics, wall paintings and a pool, located underneath the palace itself.

20K or *4c* Jaume I

Palau Reial Major

93 256 21 00 Apr–Sep Tue–Sun 10–8; Oct–Mar Tue–Sat 10–2, 4–7, Sun 10–8 Inexpensive Part of the Museu d'Història de la Ciutat (► 94)

PLAÇA REIAL

This sunny porticoed square, just off Las Ramblas, with its tall palm trees, decorative fountain and buskers was constructed in 1848. Some of the facades are decorated with terracotta reliefs of navigators and the discoverers of America, and the two tree-like central lampposts were Gaudí's first commission in Barcelona. The pretty central fountain was inspired by the *Three Graces*.

The myriad bars that line the spacious square are popular with both locals and visitors alike, especially on summer evenings. It is advisable to keep a close watch on your belongings here – the square has a reputation for shady characters and pickpockets, hence the discreet but constant police presence. On Sunday mornings a coin and stamp market is held here.

19K or *2d* Liceu, Drassanes

PLAÇA SANT JAUME

Once the hub of Roman Barcelona, this impressive square today represents the city's political heart, and is dominated by two buildings; the neoclassical and Gothic **Casa de la Ciutat** (Town Hall) and, directly opposite, the Renaissance **Palau de la Generalitat de Catalunya** (Government of Catalonia).

The origins of Barcelona's municipal authority date back to 1249, when Jaume I granted the city the right to elect councillors, giving rise to the creation of the Consell de Cent (Council of One Hundred). The famous Saló de Cent (Chamber of One Hundred) and the black marble Saló de las Cronicas (Chamber of the Chronicles) are among the architectural highlights of the Town Hall.

20K or *3c* Jaume I, Liceu

Casa de la Ciutat/Ajuntament

93 402 70 00 Sun 10–1:30 Free

Palau de la Generalitat de Catalunya

93 402 46 00 Guided tours every 30 min, 10:30–1:30 every 2nd and 4th Sun of each month

Free

PORT VELL

Although Barcelona was founded on sea-going tradition, for many years its seafront was in decay, until a major redevelopment prior to the 1992 Olympics reintegrated the Port Vell (Old Port) into the city by transforming it into a lively marina and entertainment venue. The Rambla de Mar, an undulating wooden walkway and bridge, acts as an extension of Las Ramblas, connecting the city to Port Vell's many attractions.

Maremagnum, Port Vell's biggest crowd puller, is a covered shopping and entertainment centre with chic boutiques and restaurants, currently the only Sunday shopping option in Barcelona. Adjacent to the conventional cinema complex, IMAX shows films in 3D, with state-of-the-art wrap-around screens and sound. Near by is the Aquarium (► 68), one of the biggest and best of its kind in Europe.

Take a ***golondrina*** (► 71) for a different perspective of the harbour developments. The luxurious marina, with more than 400 berths, is one of the Mediterranean's exclusive anchorages.

20L Free Drassanes, Barceloneta

Golondrinas

Moll de les Drassanes 93 442 31 06; www.lasgolondrinas.com

Times of boat trips vary according to season Moderate Drassanes

LAS RAMBLAS

Best places to see, pages 50–51.

HOTELS

Barceló Raval (€€€)
A designer hotel in the up-and-coming neighbourhood of the Raval. Rooms are sleek and contemporary with panoramic views. The rooftop pool and hip cocktail bar are a great place to unwind.
✉ Rambla del Raval 17–21 ☎ 93 320 14 90; www.barcelo.com 🚇 Liceu, Sant Antoni

Casa Camper (€€€)
Supremely hip, urban hotel run by the famous shoe company, located in a 19th-century apartment building. All rooms comprise a sleeping and separate living area.
✉ Carrer Elisabets 11 ☎ 93 342 62 80; www.casacamper.com 🚇 Liceu

Chic&Basic (€)
White, minimalist but ultimately chic, this hotel comes with all the designer trimmings, at excellent value for money.
✉ Carrer Tallers 82 ☎ 93 302 51 83; www.chicandbasic.com
🚇 Universitat

Colón (€€–€€€)
Old-fashioned, family-friendly hotel, opposite the cathedral. It has the feel of a country home rather than that of a busy city hotel.
✉ Avenida de la Catedral 7 ☎ 93 301 14 04; www.hotelcolon.es
🚇 Jaume I, Urquinaona

Hotel Denit (€)
Situated in a very quiet lane only steps from Plaça Catalunya this friendly hotel is an oasis of understated calm. All the simple, comfortable rooms have ensuite shower rooms.
✉ Carrer d'Estruc 24 ☎ 93 545 40 00; www.denit.com 🚇 Catalunya

Duques De Bergara (€€)
Recently renovated contemporary elegance in a turn-of-the-19th-century building with a pool in the courtyard of the hotel.
✉ Carrer Bergara 11 ☎ 93 301 51 51; www.hoteles-catalonia.com
🚇 Catalunya

Gat Raval and Gat Xino (€)
These two hostels are a cut above typical backpacker accommodation. They offer simple, modern, stylish rooms decorated in bold colours, WiFi access, comfortable beds and good linen.
www.gataccommodation.com
Raval ✉ Carrer Joaquín Costa 44 ☎ 93 481 66 70 🚇 Universitat
Xino ✉ Carrer Hospital 149–155 ☎ 93 324 88 33 🚇 Liceu

Gravina (€€)
This decent 3-star hotel offers a warm welcome and modern, functinal bedrooms. It has a prime location near the bustling Plaça de Catalunya.
✉ Carrer Gravina 12 ☎ 93 301 68 68; www.barcelonagravinahotel.com
🚇 Universitat

Hotel 1898 (€€€)
An historic building recently made over into the only luxury hotel right on Las Ramblas, with stylish, art deco inspired soundproofed rooms, fitness centre, state-of-the-art spa and rooftop pool.
✉ Las Ramblas 109 ☎ 93 552 95 52; www.nnhoteles.es 🚇 Catalunya

Neri (€€€)
Tucked away in the depths of the Barri Gòtic, an 18th-century palace has been converted into one of the city's best hotels, with sumptuous Asian-inspired decorations and boasting a fashionable clientele.
✉ Carrer Sant Sever 5 ☎ 93 304 06 55; www.hotelneri.com 🚇 Jaume I

Nouvel (€€)
This charming belle époque-style hotel is located on a pedestrianized shopping street just off the top of Las Ramblas, near Plaça de Catalunya. It offers old-world charm and homespun comfort.
✉ Carrer Santa Anna 18–20 ☎ 93 301 82 74; www.hotelnouvel.com
🚇 Catalunya

RESTAURANTS

Bar Lobo (€€)

Large portions of Mediterranean meals and fusion food are served here to a fashionable crowd, in a trendy two-storey locale. There are tables in the sun-trap area outside.

✉ Carrer Pintor Fortuny 3 ☎ 93 481 53 46 ⏰ Daily 1–5, 8–midnight
🚇 Liceu

Bar Ra (€)

Located just behind the colourful Boqueria market, this buzzing place is best for a light Mediterranean lunch of salad, grilled fish or pasta, especially if you can secure a place on its sun-filled terrace.

✉ Plaça de la Gardunya 3 ☎ 93 423 18 78 ⏰ Daily 10–4, 9:30–midnight
🚇 Liceu

La Bodega de Palma (€)

Another great local joint, this wood-lined *bodega* offers traditional *pá amb tomaquét* (rustic bread rubbed with tomato pulp) topped with all sorts of morsels such as sardines, vegetable omelette and a selection of local cheeses and cold meats.

✉ Carrer Palma de Sant Just 7 ☎ 93 315 06 56 ⏰ Closed Sun
🚇 Jaume I

Café de l'Academia (€€)

This is one of Barcelona's best-value restaurants, serving generous helpings of delicious Mediterranean cuisine in the heart of the old city.

✉ Carrer Lledó 1 ☎ 93 315 00 26 ⏰ Closed weekends and 2 weeks Aug
🚇 Jaume I

Can Culleretes (€€)

One of the oldest restaurants in the city (1786), traditionally decorated with wrought-iron chandeliers. Among the highlights of the Catalan cuisine on the menu is *perdiz* (partridge) stew.

✉ Carrer Quintana 5 ☎ 93 317 30 22 ⏰ Lunch: Tue–Sun 1:30–4; dinner: Tue–Sat 9–11pm; closed 3 weeks Jul 🚇 Liceu

Casa Leopoldo (€€)
Family-run seafood restaurant, in the rather run-down location of the Barri Xinés. Arrive by taxi! Its tapas bar is also hugely popular, with its barnacles, cuttlefish and baby eels.
✉ Carrer Sant Rafael 24 ☎ 93 441 30 14 ⏰ Tue–Sat 1:30–4, 9–11, Sun 1:30–4 🚇 Liceu

Dostrece (€€)
A funky little restaurant serving light Mediterranean cooking, with a handful of tables outside opposite a children's playground. There's a light informal dining room and a chill-out lounge downstairs for later in the evening.
✉ Carrer de Carme ☎ 93 301 73 06 ⏰ Daily 10–midnight
🚇 Liceu

El Gran Café (€€)
Classic restaurant, serving French and Catalan cuisine in grand turn-of-the-19th-century surroundings.
✉ Carrer d'Avinyó 9 ☎ 93 318 79 86 ⏰ Mon–Sat 🚇 Liceu

Juicy Jones (€)
Barcelona's vegans and vegetarians love this cafe for its creative, Asian-inspired dishes such as curries, dahls and other meat-free delights. It also serves fresh fruit and vegetable juices.
✉ Carrer Cardenal Casañas 7 ☎ 93 302 43 30 ⏰ Daily noon–midnight
🚇 Liceu

Kynoto (€€)
This stylish sushi bar uses the best ingredients, and serves potent cocktails. Try a Tokyo Mule.
✉ Carrer Correu Vell 8 ☎ 93 268 25 40 ⏰ Mon–Sat dinner only
🚇 Jaume I

Mam i Teca (€€)
Cutting-edge tapas and a good choice of regional dishes with a twist are served in this tiny white space. Excellent wine list.
✉ Carrer Luna 4 ☎ 93 441 33 35 ⏰ Mon, Wed–Sat 🚇 Sant Antoni

Meson David (€€)
Traditional dishes from all over Spain are served in this riotous restaurant and local institution. Try the *lechazo*, or succulent roast pork knuckle.
✉ Carrer Carretas 63 ☎ 93 441 59 34 ⏰ Tue–Sun 🚇 Drassanes

El Pla (€€)
Tucked away down a lane in the Barri Gòtic, this intimate restaurant is perfect for a romantic night out. The light, imaginative dishes are always attractively presented.
✉ Bellafilla 5 ☎ 93 412 65 52 🚇 Jaume I

Els Quatre Gats (€–€€)
Many famous artists and intellectuals used to gather in this popular *Modernista* cafe in the early 1900s. Even the menu was designed by Picasso.
✉ Carrer Montsió 3 bis ☎ 93 302 41 40 ⏰ Daily 8am–2am
🚇 Catalunya

Rita Blue (€€)
Popular bar-restaurant on a pretty Barri Gòtic square that serves Tex-Mex and Asian dishes, together with oversized margaritas, before turning into a bar-club later in the evening.
✉ Plaça Sant Agusti 3 ☎ 93 342 40 86 ⏰ Daily 8pm–1am 🚇 Liceu

Shunka (€€)
Hidden away down a side street near the cathedral this small, authentic Japanese restaurant serves excellent quality seafood. Choose your tipple from the sake menu. Reservations necessary.
✉ Carrer dels Sagristans 5 ☎ 93 412 49 91 ⏰ Tue–Sun 2–4, 8:30–11:30
🚇 Jaume I

Tallers 76 (€)
This bright, great-value place specializes in rice dishes, from paellas to simple *arroz a banda* (rice cooked in fish stock). The "continuous kitchen" makes it ideal for an early lunch or dinner.
✉ Carrer Tallers 76 ☎ 93 318 89 93 ⏰ Daily 🚇 Universitat

Taxidermista (€€)
A designer restaurant offering modern dishes such as lamb couscous or duck served with truffle vinaigrette.
✉ Plaça Reial 8 ☎ 93 412 45 36 ⏰ Closed Mon and 3 weeks Aug 🚇 Liceu

CAFES AND TAPAS BARS

Bar Pinotxo
See page 60.

El Bosc de les Fades
An extraordinary cafe-cum-magic fairy world (the name means "forest of the fairies"), decorated with fountains and princesses.
✉ Passatge de la Banca, La Rambla 4–6 ☎ 93 317 26 49 🚇 Drassanes

Café de l'Òpera
See page 58.

Café Zurich
See page 58.

Dulcina
See page 59.

Granja M Viader
See page 59.

Hard Rock Café
A prime location in the heart of the city for this world-famous chain; decorated with rock and roll memorabilia.
✉ Plaça de Catalunya 21 ☎ 93 270 23 05 🚇 Catalunya

El Jardí
In the corner of the rather neglected courtyard of the Antic Hospital de la Santa Creu, this relaxed little outdoor cafe-bar serves a choice of simple snacks and nibbles with your drink.
✉ Carrer de l'Hospital ⏰ Mon–Sat 10–11pm 🚇 Liceu

Mesón del Café
Join locals at the bar for a coffee or hot chocolate while exploring the Barri Gòric.
✉ Carrer de la Libreteria 16 ☎ 93 315 07 54 ⏰ Mon–Sat 🚇 Jaume I

Organic
There's an imaginative selection of vegan and vegetarian dishes on offer at this corner tapas bar, all prepared with local, fresh, organic produce. Take-away stall at the back of the Boqueria market and a larger refectory restaurant at Junta Comerç 11 (tel: 93 301 09 02).
✉ Carrer d'en Xuclà 15 ☎ www.antoniaorganickitchen.com ⏰ Mon–Sat 9–11pm 🚇 Liceu

La Plata
See page 60.

Taller de Tapas
See page 61.

Tres Tombs
Directly opposite the Mercat de Sant Antoni, Tres Tombs is a city institution and favourite meeting point, loved by its customers for its sun-drenched terrace and no-nonsense tapas and light snacks.
✉ Ronda Sant Antoni 11 ☎ 93 443 41 11 ⏰ Daily 🚇 Sant Antoni

SHOPPING

CLOTHES AND ACCESSORIES

Le Boudoir
Naughty but nice underwear and lingerie are displayed in this beautiful shop decorated with velvet drapery and gilt mirrors.
✉ Carrer Canuda 21 ☎ 93 302 52 81 🚇 Liceu

Calçats Solé
Handmade leather cowboy and riding boots, leather bags and sandals from Valencia, Menorca and beyond. Larger sizes of classic and casual footwear, for both men and women.
✉ Carrer Ample 7 ☎ 93 301 69 84 🚇 Drassanes

Casas Sabaters
One of several outlets in the city for this small chain of quality shoe shops stocking stylish homegrown brands including Camper and Vialis. There are extensive men's, women's and children's collections.
✉ Portal de l'Àngel ☎ 40 93 302 11 12 🚇 Catalunya

Custo Barcelona
See page 80.

Giménez y Zuazo
Women's fashions by this designer duo are fun and colourful with a range of distinctive, unusual designs and dazzling prints to chose from.
✉ Carrer Elisabets 20 ☎ 93 412 33 81 🚇 Catalunya

Mango
This branch of the international chain brims with inexpensive, trendy designs for the truly fashion conscious. There are several branches around Barcelona, include a particularly large one at Passeig de Gràcia 65 and another inside the Maremagnum shopping mall in Port Vell.
✉ Avinguda Portal de l'Àngel 7 ☎ 93 317 69 85 🚇 Catalunya

Maremagnum
At the port end of Las Ramblas across the wooden swing bridge, Maremagnum is a mall with a location. Fashion dominates, from Spanish staples such as Mango to more eclectic shoe and accessory shops. Afterwards, take in the sea views at one of the many outdoor cafes.
✉ Port Vell s/n 🕐 Daily 10–10 🚇 Drassanes

Vialis
In a city full of great shoe stores, this one stands out for its unusual styling and interesting textures and colours. They are comfortable, too.
✉ Carrer Elisabets 20 ☎ 93 342 60 71 🚇 Liceu

Zara
See page 81.

CRAFTS, ART AND DESIGN

Alamacenes de Pilar
This rambling old warehouse outlet sells beautiful shawls, combs, fans and other Spanish accessories for that authentic *señorita* look.
✉ Carrer Boqueria 43 ☎ 93 317 79 84 🚇 Liceu

Art Escudellers
See page 80.

Cereria Subirà
The oldest shop in the city of Barcelona, founded in 1761, selling candles of all sorts, ancient and modern, for both religious and purely practical purposes.
✉ Baixada Llibreteria 7 ☎ 93 315 26 06 🚇 Jaume I

Cosas de Casa
Hand-made patchwork quilts and fabrics, including the distinctive Mallorcan *roba de llengües* (literally "cloth of tongues"), striking for its red, blue or green zigzag patterns.
✉ Plaça Sant Josep Oriol 5 ☎ 93 302 73 28 🚇 Jaume I, Liceu

Germanes Garcia
Wickerwork of all shapes and sizes tumbles out of this village-style shop into the streets of the Old City.
✉ Carrer Banys Nous 15 ☎ 93 318 66 46 🚇 Liceu

El Ingenio
Children adore this old-fashioned magic shop, where party tricks are sold, and carnival masks and costumes are created in a workshop at the back. Come here for free magic shows on Thursday afternoons. A real Aladdin's cave and child's (or inner child's) delight.
✉ Carrer Rauric 6 ☎ 93 317 71 38 🚇 Liceu, Jaume I

La Manual Alpargatera
All kinds of handmade, straw-woven items are on sale , including hats, bags and their speciality, espadrilles, in every style and hue.
✉ Carrer Avinyó 7 ☎ 93 301 01 72 🚇 Liceu, Jaume I

Sala Parés
Barcelona's finest gallery specializes in 19th- and 20th-century paintings, drawings and sculptures.
✉ Carrer Pextritxol 5 ☎ 93 318 70 08 🚇 Liceu

FOOD AND DRINK

Casa Colomina
Turron, which is like nougat, from Valencia is the speciality here, sold by the slice or bar. It can made with a number of flavours. Delicious!
✉ Carrer Cucurulla 2 ☎ 93 317 46 81 🚇 Liceu

Caelum
See page 80.

Formatgeria La Seu
This old dairy now specializes in rare Spanish cheeses and olive oils, with small tables at the back so you can taste before you buy.
✉ Carrer Dagueria 16 ☎ 93 412 65 48 🚇 Jaume I

Papabubble
This old-fashioned sweet shop makes lollipops, candy canes and other sticky snacks right in front of your eyes.
✉ Carrer Ample 28 ☎ 93 268 86 25 🚇 Jaume I

MUSIC, BOOKS AND ANTIQUES

L'Arca de l'Avìa
A treasure trove of antique cottons, linens, silks. Beautiful, albeit pricey, patchwork eiderdowns and beaded bags can be found here.
✉ Carrer Banys Nous 20 ☎ 93 302 15 98 🚇 Liceu

Artur Ramon Anticuario
A wide array of antique paintings, sculpture and decorative arts.
Carrer de la Palla 25 93 302 59 70 Jaume I

Casa Beethoven
Founded in 1915, this shop has scores and sheet music, specializing in pieces by Spanish and Catalan composers.
La Rambla 97 93 301 48 26 Liceu

Castelló
A chain of record shops. Carrer Tallers 3 has a huge selection of pop, rock, jazz, blues and soul. No 7 is devoted to classical music.
Carrer Tallers 3 & 7 93 302 59 46 Catalunya

La Central
Enormous, two-storey bookshop with a large section of English-language literature, a good choice of art books and a lovely cafe.
Carrer Elisabets 6 93 317 02 93 Catalunya

FNAC
A book megastore inside El Triangle shopping mall. Books, DVDs, CDs, computers, PlayStations, computer games and magazines.
El Triangle, Plaça de Catalunya 93 344 18 00 Mon–Sat 10–10
Catalunya

Jordi Capell – Cooperative d'Arquitectes
Specialist bookshop for architecture and design, in the basement of the College of Architects.
Plaça Nova 5 93 481 35 60 Jaume I, Liceu

ENTERTAINMENT

City Hall
Just near the Plaça Catalunya, this established dance club is guaranteed to be full any night of the week. Music changes from funk on weeknights to heavy-duty techno at weekends.
Rambla Catalunya 2–4 93 317 21 77 Daily midnight–5am
Catalunya

Club Fellini
A hugely popular dance club right on Las Ramblas, pulling in a mixed crowd of locals, students and tourists.
Las Ramblas 27 93 272 49 80 Daily midnight–5am Drassanes

Gran Teatre del Liceu
World-famous singers, including the Catalan diva Montserrat Caballé, have performed here.
Las Ramblas 51–59 93 485 99 13; www.liceubarcelona.com Liceu

Harlem Jazz Club
Small, but very atmospheric jazz club – a favourite of jazz aficionados.
Carrer Comtessa de Sobradiel 8 93 310 07 55 Tue–Sun 8pm–4am Jaume I

Jamboree
A choice nightspot for blues, soul, jazz, funk and occasional hip-hop live bands. Upstairs is a laid-back bar with Spanish music.
Plaça Reial 93 301 75 64 Daily 9pm–5am; live gigs start at 11pm Liceu

La Macarena
Dark and steamy disco club that pulls in an energetic crowd.
Carrer Nou de Sant Francesc 5 93 302 45 93 Mon–Sat midnight–5am Drassanes

Marsella
A traditional bar in the Barri Xines, run by the same family for five generations, serving locally made *absenta* (absinthe).
Carrer Sant Pau 65 93 442 72 63 Mon–Thu 10pm–2:30am, Fri–Sun 10pm–3:30am Liceu

Moog
The place to head for if you feel the need for a night of electronic dance music. The upstairs room plays more diverse dance tunes.
Carrer Arc del Teatre 3 93 301 72 82 Drassanes

La Ribera to Port Olímpic

La Ribera, one of the oldest districts of Barcelona, has become home to buzzing *tapas* bars, wine bars and stylish restaurants situated in Gothic palaces. It also has the city's most eclectic shopping opportunities, a handful of hotels and some of the swankiest nightclubs.

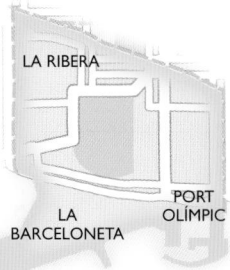

The northern half of the district, Sant Pere, contains the Modernist masterpiece Palau de la Música Catalana. Carrer de Montcada, in the Born, is now a showcase of art galleries and museums, including the Museu Picasso, one of the city's biggest attractions. The lanes around Carrer de Montcada are full of fashion boutiques and workshops where jewellers and potters carry on their trade much as they did in medieval times.

Passeig del Born, the main thoroughfare through the Born district, is a lively promenade lined with restaurants and cocktail bars. Here you'll find the Basílica de Santa Maria del Mar, known as the merchant's cathedral. A pleasant waterfront walk leads from La Ribera around the fishing village of Barceloneta to the popular beaches *(platjas)* on either side of Port Olímpic.

LA BARCELONETA AND LES PLATJAS

Following the siege and conquest of Barcelona by Felipe V in 1714, a large area of the Ribera district was destroyed to make way for a new citadel. The displaced residents lived for years in makeshift shelters on the beach, until in 1755 a new district was developed on a triangular wedge of reclaimed land between the harbour and the sea, named La Barceloneta (Little Barcelona).

In the 19th century, La Barceloneta became home to seamen and dockers and it is still a working district, retaining its shanty-town atmosphere, fishy smells and a quayside lined with the boats. Today visitors come here to eat in the fine seafood cafes and restaurants and enjoy the beaches *(platjas)*.

Thanks to 20 years of regeneration, Barcelona is now bordered by a long strip of blonde sand dotted with beach bars, restaurants and marinas. Seven beaches *(platjas)* stretch over 4km (2.5 miles) starting from the promontory marked by the controversial new landmark, the W hotel (▶ 121) at the end of Barceloneta. Closest to the centre of town, San Sebastià and Barceloneta are understandably the busiest, backed by traditional paella restaurants and stylish new bars. The sections around the Port Olímpic are also very popular, not least as they're closest to a metro station.

21L (Barceloneta), 21M (Les Platjas)

Barceloneta, Ciutadella-Vila Olímpica, Poble Nou

Barceloneta: 17, 36, 39, 40, 45, 57, 59, 64, 157. Les Platjas: 10, 17, 39, 45, 57, 59, 71, 92, 157

DISSENY HUB MONTCADA (DHUB)

The Disseny Hub is the city-centre temporary exhibition space for the design museums based in the Palau Reial de Pedralbes (► 158). It occupies a beautiful 14th-century palace opposite the Picasso Museum (► 46–47). The quality of the architecture and design exhibitions is always high and there is usually one with free entrance.

www.dhub-bcn.cat

21K ✉ Carrer Montcada 12 ☎ 93 256 23 00 ⏰ Tue–Sat 10–7, Sun and public hols 10–8; free on Sun after 3pm 💶 Moderate 🍴 Cafe-restaurant (€) 🚇 Jaume I, Barceloneta

MUSEU D'HISTÒRIA DE CATALUNYA

Thanks to the influence of the Olympic Games, and the opening up of the old port as a leisure area, the Palau de Mar (Palace of the Sea) – an impressive late 19th-century warehouse – became the centrepiece of a harbourside development that includes a promenade, restaurants and marina. It houses the Museu d'Història de Catalunya (Museum of Catalan History).

This is one of Barcelona's most interactive museums, opened in 1996. Some critics have dubbed it a "theme park", because of its lack of original exhibits, but it is nevertheless a dynamic and stimulating museum, covering the history of Catalonia, from prehistoric times to the present day, in an entertaining fashion, through state-of-the-art displays, films, special effects and audio-visual technology – tread an Arab

waterwheel, mount a cavalier's charger, drive an early tram, take cover in a Civil War air-raid shelter…

The museum is divided into seven sections, each presenting an in-depth picture of the economy, politics, technology, culture and everyday life of Catalonia over the centuries: the region's prehistory, the consolidation of Catalonia in the Middle Ages, its maritime role, links with the Austrian Empire in the 16th and 17th centuries, economic growth and industrialization, the 1936 Civil War and the repression of Catalonia under Franco, through to the restoration of democracy in 1979. The museum gives an insight into the complexities of this "nation within a nation".

www.mhcat.net

21L Plaça Pau Vila 3, Port Vell 93 225 47 00 Tue–Sat 10–7, Wed 10–8, Sun and public hols 10–2:30 Inexpensive; free 1st Sun of month Rooftop cafe (€) Barceloneta Gift shop, temporary exhibitions

MUSEU PICASSO

Best places to see, pages 46–47.

PALAU DE LA MÚSICA CATALANA

In a city bursting with architectural wonders, the Palau de la Música Catalana (Palace of Catalan Music) – commissioned by the Orfeó Català (Catalan Musical Society) in 1904 and created by local architect Lluís Domènech i Montaner between 1905 and 1908 – stands out as one of Barcelona's greatest masterpieces and a symbol of the renaissance of Catalan culture. In 1997 it was declared a World Heritage Site by UNESCO.

The bare brick facade is highlighted with colourful ceramic pillars, fancy windows and busts of Palestrina, Bach, Beethoven and Wagner. The sculptural group projecting from the corner of the building represents popular song. A balcony runs around the building and the main structure is supported by ornate columns that form huge dramatic archways over the entrance.

The interior continues the ornamental theme with a profusion of decoration in the entrance hall, foyer and staircase – almost overpowering in its attention to detail. The pièce de résistance, however, must be the concert hall, with its exquisite roof (an inverted cupola made of stained glass), its sculptures, ceramics and paintings dedicated to musical muses (including Josep Anselm Clavé, the great 19th-century reviver of Catalan music), and its beautiful balconies and columns, designed to enhance the perspective of the auditorium.

The Palau offers a varied programme where choral and classic music are supplemented by concerts, world music events and top-quality flamenco. Do your best to get tickets for a show; the acoustics are excellent. Alternatively, visit the building on one of the tours which run several times a day. The auditorium is usually included although not when there is a rehearsal in progress.

www.palaumusica.org

21J Sant Pere més Alt 2 90 244 28 82 Public areas daily 9am–midnight Expensive Cafe (€) Urquinaona 17, 19, 40, 45 English-language guided tours daily. Purchase tickets from box office or the adjacent gift shop.

ANY . MCMIX

PARC DE LA CIUTADELLA

This delightful walled park is a haven of shade and tranquillity just a stone's throw from the old city and waterfront. What's more, hidden among the trees, lawns, promenades and a boating lake, you'll find the Parc Zoològic (► 69) and a host of other attractions.

In 1888 the park was the site of the Universal Exposition and still contains some impressive relics of that great fair, including the red-brick Castle of Three Dragons, a stupendous mock-medieval fortress designed by the *Modernist* architect Lluís Domènech i Montaner as the exhibition cafe; currently closed to the public. The L'Umbracle, a fanciful iron-and-glass vivarium, and the L'Hivernacle also date from this time. The main showpiece of the park is the Font Monumental – a huge, neoclassical-style fountain, smothered in allegorical sculptures.

22K ✉ Main entrance: Passeig Lluís Companys Free Ciutadella, Arc de Triomf, Barceloneta, Jaume I

PORT OLÍMPIC

Port Olímpic was created for the 1992 Olympic Games and it has become a lively nightspot, with restaurants, bars (with outdoor terraces in summer) and clubs around its promenades and a glittering yachting marina. A striking bronze fish sculpture by Frank Gehry (architect of the Guggenheim Museum in Bilbao) towers over the Passeig Marítim, which links the marina with Barceloneta and then extends 8km (5miles) in the opposite direction to Sant Adrià del Besòs.

23M ✉ Port Olímpica Ciutadella 36, 45, 59

SANTA MARIA DEL MAR

Best places to see, pages 54–55.

HOTELS

Arts Barcelona (€€€)
Hotel Arts Barcelona towers above the entrance to the Port Olímpic signposted by vast copper fish designed by Frank Gehry. This state-of-the-art hotel provides unabashed luxury beside the sea, and has an open-air pool and a spa.
✉ Carrer de la Marina 19–21 ☎ 93 221 10 00; www.ritzcarlton.com
🚇 Ciutadella-Vila Olímpica

Banys Orientals (€–€€)
A stylish hotel that mixes taste with function at unbeatable prices. In a great location on a pedestrian street in the charming Born neighbourhood. Reserve ahead.
✉ Argentería, 37 ☎ 932 68 84 60; www.hotelbanysorientals.com
🚇 Jaume I

Hotel 54 (€€€)
Bright, modern hotel in Barceloneta with fine views over the yachts in the Port Vell marina. The rooms are considerately soundproofed from the restaurants below.
✉ Passeig Joan de Borbó 54 ☎ 93 225 00 54; www.hotel54barceloneta.com
🚇 Barceloneta

W Barcelona (€€€)
All the latest luxuries include a Bliss spa, seaside pool, rooftop bar and top-class restaurant at this monolithic building rising out of the waves at the very tip of Barceloneta.
✉ Placa de la Rosa dels Vents, 1, Passeig de Joan de Borbo ☎ 932 95 28 00; www.starwoodhotels.com 🚇 Barceloneta

RESTAURANTS

Agua (€€)
Located right on Barceloneta beach, near Port Olímpic. The menu is creative, yet offers excellent traditional Barceloneta fare, with the emphasis on rice-based dishes. Sunday lunchtime is popular.
✉ Passeig Marítim de la Barceloneta 30 ☎ 93 225 12 72 🕐 Daily 1–4, 8–midnight (closes 1pm Fri, Sat) 🚇 Ciutadella-Vila Olímpica

Bestial (€€)
This fabulous Italian restaurant is right on the beach, with extensive wood decking, palm trees and parasol-topped tables.
✉ Passeig Marítim 32 ☎ 93 224 04 07 ⏲ Daily 🚇 Ciutadella-Vila Olímpica

La Bombeta (€)
A genuine, old-school tapas bar worth seeking out. The speciality is *bombas*, huge fluffy potato balls smothered in spicy *brava* sauce.
✉ Carrer Maquinista 3 ☎ 93 319 94 45 ⏲ Thu–Tue 🚇 Barceloneta

Cal Pinxo (€€€)
Cal Pinxo serves spot-on traditional dishes like crunchy *chiperones* and the house-speciality monkfish *(rape)*, with sea views. The nearby sister restaurant is a little calmer with marina views.
✉ Carrer de Baluard 124, Barceloneta ☎ 93 221 50 28; www. pinxoplatja.com ⏲ Tue–Sun 🚇 Barceloneta
✉ Palau de Mar, Port Vell ☎ 93 221 22 11; www.calpintxo.com ⏲ Closed Mon 🚇 Barceloneta

Can Majó (€€€)
See page 62.

Comerç 24 (€€€)
One of the leading names in New Catalan Cuisine, Carles Abellan redefines classic Spanish dishes, with combinations, textures and flavours that delight. Try the *festa de tapas* (tasting menu).
✉ Carrer Comerç 24 ☎ 93 319 21 02 ⏲ Tue–Sat 🚇 Jaume I

Cuines Santa Caterina (€–€€)
Open kitchens use produce from the adjoining market for dishes ranging from *butifarra amb mongets* (sausage with white beans) to well-executed sushi as well as excellent vegetarian options.
✉ Mercat Santa Caterina, Avinguda Francesc Cambó 16 ☎ 93 268 9918; www.grupotragaluz.com/santacaterina ⏲ Tue–Sun 🚇 Jaume I

El Lobito (€€€)
See page 62.

Els Fogons de la Barceloneta (€€)
See page 62.

La Mar Salada (€€–€€€)
Friendly service and a mix of traditional and creative cooking make this the best of the options on this marina-fronted strip.
✉ Passeig de Joan de Borbó 58 ☎ 93 221 21 27; www.lamarsalada.cat
⏰ Daily 🚇 Barceloneta

La Paradeta (€–€€)
Self-service restaurant with great food and affordable prices. Fresh seafood is cooked simply. Credit cards not accepted.
✉ Carrer de Comercial 7 ☎ 93 268 19 39 ⏰ Tue–Sat 8–11:30am, Sat, Sun 1–4 🚇 Arc de Triomf

Sal Cafè (€€)
On the waterfront promenade, Sal Cafè offers Mediterranean cuisine as bright as its surroundings. Reserve ahead for an outdoor table to take in the sea view under an orange umbrella.
✉ Passeig Marítimo de la Barceloneta s/n ☎ 93 224 07 07 ⏰ Sun–Wed 1:30–4, Thu–Sat 1:30–4, 8:30–midnight 🚇 Barceloneta

Set Portes (€€€)
See page 63.

Torre de Alt Mar (€€€)
See page 63.

CAFÉS AND TAPAS BARS

Cal Pep
See page 60.

DHUB Cafe
See page 58.

Euskal Etxea
See page 60.

Laie Museu Picasso
See page 59

Origins 99.9%
This is the original and prettiest of a chain of cafes using Catalan-only ingredients. Cakes, sandwiches and salads are all top quality and there is a shop selling cheeses and other local specialities.
✉ Carrer Vidrería 6–8 ☎ 93 310 75 31 ⏰ Daily 🚇 Jaume I

Santa Marta
See page 59.

Schilling
Spacious cafe and bar popular with a gay clientele and oozing understated elegance.
✉ Carrer Ferran 23 ☎ 93 317 67 87 🚇 Liceu

Taller de Tapas
See page 61.

Vasa de Oro
See page 61.

La Vinya del Senyor
Tiny, stand-up wine bar, with outside terraces, beside Santa Maria del Mar.
✉ Plaça Santa Maria 5 ☎ 93 310 33 79 ⏰ Tue–Sun 🚇 Jaume I

El Xampanyet
See page 61

SHOPPING

CLOTHES AND ACCESSORIES

Alea
Showcase for up-and-coming Catalan jewellers in La Ribera with many more designers working in the labyrinth of streets near by.
✉ Carrer Argenteria 66 ☎ 93 310 13 73 🚇 Jaume I, Barceloneta

Custo Barcelona
See page 80.

On-Land
Highly fashionable yet ultimately wearable clothing for men and women from Spanish designers.
Carrer Princesa 25 93 310 02 11 Jaume I

FOOD AND DRINK

La Botifarreria
A huge selection of Catalan sausages ranging from traditional recipes with mushrooms to curried apple or Roquefort cheese.
Carrer de Santa Maria 4 93 319 91 23; www.labotifarreria.com
Jaume I

Brunells Patisseria
Appears in the *Guinness Book of Records* for making Spain's biggest Easter egg. Try the *torró* (traditional almond fudge), *roques de Montserrat* (meringues) and *carquinyolis* (soft almond biscuits).
Carrer Montcada 7 93 319 68 25 Jaume I

Bubo
These jewel-like creations are some of the most desirable cakes and petit fours imaginable.
Caputexes 10 93 268 72 24; www.bubo.ws Jaume I

Casa Gispert
Sells dried fruits, spices, cocoa, coffee and nuts which are toasted daily in a traditional oak-fired oven.
Carrer Sombrerers 23 93 319 75 35 Jaume I

Mercat de Santa Caterina
A mouthwatering selection of fresh produce available in the stunning market restyled by the architect Enric Miralles.
Avinguda de Francesc Cambó 16 93 319 57 40; www.mercatsantacaterina.net Mon 7:30–2:30, Tue, Wed, Sat 7:30–3:30, Thu, Fri 7:30–8:30pm Jaume I

La Ribera
Eye-popping array of olives and salted cod as well as top-class conserves or tins of anchovies, mussels and the like.
Plaça Comercial 11 93 319 52 06; www.laribera-sa.es Jaume I

Vila Viniteca
These leading wine sellers are equally helpfully offering advice on a bottle for a picnic or arranging for a shipment home.
Carrer Agullers 7 93 232 77 77; www.vilaviniteca.es Jaume I

ENTERTAINMENT

CDLC
Owned by the Barça football team, one of the most exclusive (and expensive) clubs in the city. Dance floor, terrace and restaurant.
Passeig Maritim 32 93 224 04 70 Daily until 3am Ciutadella-Vila Olímpica

Club Catwalk
Two separate dance floors, one playing house and the other R&B and hip hop. Expect celebrity DJs and a hefty admission.
Carrer Ramon Trias Fargas s/n 93 221 61 61 Thu–Sat until 5am Ciutadella-Vila Olímpica

Gimlet
An established cocktail bar popular for its New York vibe, jazz soundtrack and excellently mixed drinks.
Carrer Rec 24 93 310 10 27 Closed Sun Jaume I

Mix
Fashionable bar-club with stylish decor and clientele to match. Live jazz on Wednesday and DJs other nights of the week.
Carrer Comerç 21 93 319 46 96 Daily until 3am Jaume I

Palau de la Música Catalana
Barcelona's main venue for classical music (➤ 118–119).
Carrer Sant Francesc de Paula 2 93 295 72 00; www.palaumusica.org
Box office: Mon–Fri 10–9, Sat 3–9

The Eixample and Gràcia

At the heart of the Eixample is the famed 'Golden Square', an area of elegant streets lined with *Modernista* architecture ranging from private homes to public buildings, two of them by Gaudí: Casa Milà and Casa Batlló. The Eixample is also where you will find Gaudí's amazing unfinished La Sagrada Família, one of the city's most celebrated sights. The streets of Barcelona's grid also offer many top hotels, plus smart restaurants and shops.

Gràcia, once an outlying village, is now a picturesque suburb. It is home to students, artists and writers and its atmosphere, narrow streets and shady squares with funky bars contrast sharply with the orderly grid plan of Eixample. Gràcia also has a building by Gaudí – Casa Vicens and up on the hills above is his celebrated Parc Güell.

CASA ASIA

This sumptous *Modernista* mansion by Doménech i Montaner houses Barcelona's Asian cultural centre, which hosts regular exhibitions making it well worth a visit. These can range from ancient Tibetan art and craft to Vietnamese propaganda posters and the work of Asian photographers, and are heightened by their magnificent setting. Every September Casa Asia organizes the Festival Asia, which invites Asian artists and performers to the city.

www.casaasia.es

8F Avinguda Diagonal 373 93 368 08 36 Tue–Sat 10–8, Sun 10–2 Free Snack bar Diagonal

CASA MILÀ (LA PEDRERA)

Best places to see, pages 36–37.

L'EIXAMPLE

L'Eixample means 'The Extension' in Catalan, and this district was laid out between 1860 and 1920 to expand the city beyond its medieval walls and link it with outlying municipalities.

The innovative plan, drawn up by civil engineer Ildefons Cerdà, broke with the tradition of Spanish urban planning, with its geometric grid of streets running parallel to the seafront. The aptly named Avinguda Diagonal cuts through at 45 degrees to add a touch of originality. The utopian features of Cerdà's plan have been largely forgotten, and today many people dislike its monotony while others praise its visionary urban planning.

The Eixample consists of two *barris*: *L'Esquerra* (The Left) is more residential, whereas *La Dreta* (The Right) contains the *Modernista* landmarks Casa Milà, the three properties of La Manzana de la Discòrdia, the Fundació Antoni Tàpies, the Hospital de la Santa Creu i Sant Pau and La Sagrada Família. Chic boutiques line its streets and, at night, its stylish bars and nightclubs come alive.

19G Catalunya, Diagonal, Entença, Girona, Hospital Clinic, Passeig de Gràcia, Provença, Tetuan, Vergaguer, Universitat

FUNDACIÓ ANTONI TÀPIES

The Tàpies Foundation was established by Catalan artist Antoni Tàpies in 1984 to promote the study and understanding of modern art. It is housed in the former Montaner i Simon publishing house, built by Lluis Domènech i Montaner between 1880 and 1889. The striking *Mudejar*-style facade is crowned by an eye-catching piece of art made of wire and tubing by Tàpies, *Cloud and Chair* (1990). Inside, there is an exhaustive library documenting art and artists of the 20th century, and one of the most complete collections of Tàpies' own works, plus good-quality temporary exhibitions.

www.fundaciotapies.org

20G Carrer d'Aragó 255 93 487 03 15 Tue–Sun 10–8

Moderate, children under 16 free 7, 16, 17, 20, 22, 24, 28, 39, 43, 44

Passeig de Gràcia Library and small bookshop

GRÀCIA

In 1820, Gràcia was a mere village of about 2,500 inhabitants. By 1897, the population had swollen to 61,000, making it the ninth-largest city in Spain, known as a radical centre of Catalanism and anarchism. This is reflected in some street names – Mercat de la Llibertat and Plaça de la Revolució. Since then, Gràcia has been engulfed by the expanding city, yet even now it maintains a village-like, no-frills, bohemian atmosphere and the *Graciencs* still call the cityfolk *Barcelonins*.

There are no real 'tourist' attractions here, except Gaudí's first major commission, Casa Vicens (Carrer de les Carolines 24), still a private home. Gràcia's real appeal is its muddle of narrow atmospheric streets and squares, including the Plaça del Sol, an ideal place to stop for a coffee and watch the world go by. The Plaça de la Virreina and the Plaça de la Vila de Gràcia are two of the oldest squares. You'll also find great shopping along the Carrer Verdi and a concentration of reasonably priced bars and restaurants in Gràcia.

9E Fontana, Gràcia, Joanic

Festa Major every August (➤ 25)

HOSPITAL DE LA SANTA CREU I SANT PAU

This remarkable hospital complex is a masterpiece of *Modernisme* by innovative architect Lluís Domènech i Montaner. Not only did he deliberately defy the orderliness of the Eixample by aligning the buildings at 45 degrees to the street grid, but he also built the complex in contravention of established hospital concepts by creating a "hospital-village" of 48 small pavilions connected by underground passages and surrounded by gardens, rather than one single massive building.

Construction began in 1902, as a replacement for the old hospital in the Raval, and the new hospital was inaugurated in 1930. The main pavilion, with its graceful tower and ornate mosaic facade, serves as a majestic entrance to the whole ensemble. Inside, the various pavilions are grouped around gardens that occupy an area equivalent to nine blocks of the Eixample, where both doctors and patients alike enjoyed a peaceful natural environment. The pavilions are decorated in ornate *Modernista* style using brick, colourful ceramics and natural stone.

The complex was declared a UNESCO World Cultural Heritage site in 1984 but can no longer meet the needs of the modern hospital, which is being relocated. It is being refurbished to reopen as the International Centre of the Mediterranean.

www.rutadelmodernisme.com

12E Carrer de Sant Antoni Maria Claret 167–171 90 207 66 21 Guided tours in English Mon–Thu 10:15 and 12:15 Moderate; grounds free Small coffee shop in one of the pavilions (€) Hospital de Sant Pau Part of the complex will be closed to visitors during restoration

MANZANA DE LA DISCORDIA

Casa Amatller

This is the first of three houses that have striking *Modernista* facades and are collectively known as the Manzana de la Discordia. Chocolate manufacturer Antonio Amatller i Costa commissioned Josep Puig i Cadafalch to remodel Casa Amatller into an extravagant home with a neo-Gothic facade decorated with sculptures, coats of arms and floral reliefs, and crowned by a stepped gable. Inside the broad entranceway, the beautiful wooden elevator was one of the earliest to be installed in Barcelona. Note also the amazing carvings on one interior doorway depicting animals making chocolate. To see inside the building you will need to take a guided tour, which includes an opportunity to taste Amatller chocolate.

www.amatller.org

20G Passeig de Gràcia 41 93 487 72 17 Guided tours Mon–Fri at 11, 12 and 1. Advance reservations necessary Expensive Passeig de Gràcia There is a short, free photographic introduction to the house through the gift shop beyond the entrance hall

Casa Batlló

Casa Batlló is one of the most famous buildings of the *Modernista* school, designed by Gaudí for Josep Batlló i Casanovas and completed in 1907. The seductive building is an undulating creation of glazed ceramics and sculpted forms. Some say the mosaic facade represents Sant Jordi's (Saint George's) triumph over the dragon while others claim it is a seascape of scaly creatures and whalebone balconies. A visit to the interior gives a comprehensive tour of the building and into Gaudí's designs, and takes in the main apartment, the attic and roof terrace.

www.casabatllo.es

20G Passeig de Gràcia 43 93 216 03 06 Daily 9–8 Expensive Passeig de Gràcia

Casa Lleó-Morera

This striking building is considered Lluís Domènech i Montaner's most exuberant decorative work. Its flamboyant facade cleverly minimizes its corner plot by placing visual emphasis on the distinctive ornate circular balconies, columned galleries and oriel windows. Inside, a florid pink mosaic vestibule and open staircase lead to first-floor living quarters, which are lavishly decorated with stencilled stuccowork, stained glass, marquetry and mosaics, portraying roses (the nationalist symbol of Catalonia), lions *(lleó)* and mulberry bushes *(morera)* which give this house its name. The interior is closed to the public, but the exterior is well worth a visit.

20G Passeig de Gràcia 35 No phone Interior not open to the public Passeig de Gràcia

MUSEU EGIPCI DE BARCELONA

Although some of the pieces in the expansive Egyptian collection belonging to the owner of the Derby Hotels can be seen in the Hotel Balmes (➤ 139), the bulk of them are here at this impressive museum. From beautifully carved sarcophagi to everyday utensils, sculpture, jewellery and mummified animals, the well-ordered exhibits are spread out over two floors of this pretty Eixample mansion and span more than 3,000 years of fascinating Egyptian culture. There is a programme of temporary exhibitions.

There are special night visits during summer during in which actors dressed in full Egyptian regalia perform scenes from Cleopatra's life, ending in a banquet held on the rear terrace.

www.museuegipci.com

20G Carrer Valencia 284 93 488 01 88 Mon–Sat 10–8, Sun 10–2 Expensive Passeig de Gràcia, Diagonal Book and gift shop

PARC DE LA CREUETA DEL COLL

This park was built in a former quarry by Olympic architects Martorell and Mackay in 1987. Surrounded by dramatic cliff-faces, it is scattered with modern sculptures and wooded pathways. The shallow, tiled swimming pool is popular with children in summer.

10B Passeig Mare de Déu del Coll Daily 10–dusk Free
25, 28, 87

PARK GÜELL

Best places to see, pages 48–49.

LA SAGRADA FAMÍLIA

Best places to see, pages 52–53.

TORRE AGBAR

Barcelona's brazen new structure is a colourful landmark on the skyline. Built for the local water company by French architect Jean Nouvel, the Torre Agbar features an ingenious aluminium 'skin' that ripples with light at night in hues of green, blue and red.

www.torreagbar.com

24H (off map) Plaça de les Glorías s/n Glorías 7, 56, 60, 92, 192

HOTELS

Hotel Balmes (€€)
This great little hotel offers comfort and a rear garden with a pool, a real rarity for a 3-star hotel. It's located within walking distance of the Passeig de Gràcia shopping strip and all the major sites.
✉ Carrer Mallorca 216 ☎ 93 451 19 14; www.derbyhotels.com 🚇 Diagonal

Condes De Barcelona (€€€)
A stylish hotel that puts you right at the heart of Barcelona's main shopping district. Elegant public rooms, and bedrooms furnished in *Modernista* style.
✉ Passeig de Gràcia 73–75 ☎ 93 445 00 00 🚇 Diagonal

Hostal Goya (€)
A friendly, family-run option close to Plaça Catalunya. Tastefully decorated, comfortable rooms in this Eixample townhouse.
✉ Pau Claris 74 ☎ 93 302 25 65, www.hostalgoya.com 🚇 Catalunya, Urquinaona

Omm (€€€)
The city's most fashionable hotel, with a rooftop plunge pool and Moo, a cutting-edge restaurant in the foyer. The monochrome rooms are cleverly designed to adapt to your needs, with movable storage space and light that you manipulate to suit your mood.
✉ Carrer Rosselló 265 ☎ 93 445 40 00; www.hotelomm.es 🚇 Diagonal

Praktik (€)
A fresh modern *hostal* offering very good-value a couple of blocks from the Passig de Gràcia. Crisp, contemporary rooms.
✉ Diputació 325 ☎ 93 467 32 87; www.praktikhotels.com 🚇 Girona, Passeig de Gràcia

Praktik Rambla (€€–€€€)
A very comfortable boutique hotel in a splendid *Modernista* building with contemporary design touches. Sunny terrace.
✉ Rambla Catalunya 27 ☎ 93 343 66 90; www.hotelpraktikrambla.com
🚇 Catalunya, Passeig de Gràcia

5 Rooms (€€)
There's a friendly informal atmosphere in this *Modernista* apartment steps from the Passeig de Gràcia. Attractive rooms, suites and apartments available.
✉ Carrrer de Pau Claris 72 ☎ 93 342 78 80; www.thefiverooms.com
🚇 Catalunya, Urquinanoa

RESTAURANTS

Amélie (€)
It's hard to beat an outside table in the sun at this relaxed restaurant-bar on Gràcia's main square. There's an extensive menu of snacks but the lunchtime menu of international cuisine with South American touches is particularly good value.
✉ Plaça de la Vila de Gràcia 11 ☎ 93 513 37 46 🕐 Tue–Sun 🚇 Joanic, Fontana

Alkimia (€€€)
See page 62.

Beltxenea (€€€)
Barcelona's premier Basque restaurant is set in an elegant 19th-century *Modernista* building, with a pretty interior garden terrace.
✉ Carrer Mallorca 275 ☎ 93 215 30 24 🕐 Mon–Fri lunch, dinner, Sat dinner only 🚇 Diagonal, Passeig de Gràcia

Botafumeiro (€€€)
Fish is flown in daily from Galicia for this seafood restaurant. The *mariscos Botafumeira* (seafood platter) is a sight to behold.
✉ Carrer de Gran de Gràcia 81 ☎ 93 218 42 30 🕐 Daily 1pm–1am
🚇 Fontana

Casa Calvet (€€€)
See page 62.

Cinc Sentits (€€€)
See page 62.

Dragonfly (€€)
This stylish place evokes Old Shanghai, with sepia photographs and other oriental paraphernalia. Peking duck and dim sum.
✉ Carrer València 232 ☎ 93 451 11 28 ⏲ Mon–Sat lunch, dinner, Sun lunch only 🚇 Diagonal, Passieg de Gràcia

Flash Flash (€€)
The genuine 1970s decor is a real draw to this popular eatery specializing in *tortillas* (omelettes – try the truffle omelette for something exotic) and truly great burgers.
✉ Carrer Granada de Penedès 25 ☎ 93 237 09 90 ⏲ Daily 🚇 FGC Gràcia

Mé (€€)
This unusual restaurant fuses Vietnamese and Creole cuisines into startling dishes such as "firecracker" prawns. The soft jazz soundtrack and cocktail list give the place a slick, bistro-type feel.
✉ Carrer Paris 162 ☎ 93 419 49 33 ⏲ Thu–Sat dinner only; closed Sun, Mon 🚇 Diagonal

La Miafanera (€€)
This stylish eatery specializes in rice dishes from Asian 'sticky rices' to Italian risotto. Try the well-priced tasting menu.
✉ Carrer Sagués 16 ☎ 93 240 59 12 ⏲ Tue–Sat 🚌 7, 33, 34

Moments (€€€)
See page 63.

Le Relais de Venise (€€)
This classic French restaurant, seemingly unchanged since the 1950s, serves only entrecôte and pomme frites, but the quality and service make up for lack of choice. Leave room for dessert.
✉ Carrer Pau Claris 142 ☎ 93 467 21 62 ⏲ Daily 🚇 Passeig de Gràcia

Tragaluz (€€)
A good place to tempt your taste buds with New Catalan Cuisine, which uses local ingredients in inventive ways.
✉ Pasaje de la Concepción 5 ☎ 93 487 01 96 ⏲ Daily 🚇 Diagonal

CAFES AND TAPAS BARS

La Bodegueta

An old-school wine tavern that is well known for its charcuterie and local wines.

✉ Rambla de Catalunya 100 ☎ 93 215 48 94 ⏰ Daily, closed Sun lunch 🚇 Provença

Cerveceria Catalana

See page 60.

Pasteleria Mauri

See page 59.

Tapaç 24 (€€)

See page 61.

SHOPPING

CLOTHES, JEWELLERY AND ACCESSORIES

Adolfo Domínguez

Adolfo Domínguez is one of Spain's most successful fashion designers. Stylish, highly wearable clothing for men, women and children.

✉ Passeig de Gràcia 32 ☎ 93 487 41 70 🚇 Passeig de Gràcia

Bagués

An old family of gold and silversmiths' shop on the ground floor of the striking Casa Amatller (➤ 134) contains priceless works by Masriera, the sole creator of the *Modernista* style in the Spanish jewellery trade.

✉ Passeig de Gràcia 41 ☎ 93 216 01 73; www.bagues.com 🚇 Passeig de Gràcia

Contribuciones y Moda

Large fashion outlet store for men and women selling last year's high-fashion labels at great prices. Upstairs has more everyday wear, from mainly Spanish brands.

✉ Carrer de Sant Miquel 30 ☎ 93 218 71 40 🚇 Diagonal

Desigual
The fresh and funky street and urban wear from this local label is known for bold, dramatic prints and quirky styling.
✉ Passeig de Gràcia 7 Passeig de Gràcia

Joaquín Berao
Jewellery by Joaquín Berao, celebrated for his unusual combinations of materials and avant-garde chunky designs.
✉ Rambla de Catalunya 74 ☎ 93 215 00 91 Diagonal

Limobebe
Wonderful rainbow collection of the coolest cotton basics for babies and young children. Well-chosen toys and baby equipment.
✉ Rambla de Prat 9 ☎ 90 255 08 83; www.limobebe.com Fontana

Loewe
See page 80.

Lydia Delgado
Delgado is one of Barcelona's most distinctive local designers of elegant, easy-to-wear women's fashions.
✉ Carrer Minerva 21 ☎ 93 415 99 98 Gràcia, Diagonal

Muxart Chic
This is a vibrant shop showcasing shoes by Barcelonan shoe designer, Muxart.
✉ Rambla de Catalunya 47 ☎ 93 467 74 23 Passeig de Gràcia

Nobodinoz
For trendy kids, and their parents, this beautiful concept store sells designer clothing, toys and knick-knacks for the young ones.
✉ Carrer Séneca 9 ☎ 93 368 63 35 Diagonal

Regia
Barcelona's prime perfumery. It has its own small "Perfume Museum" at the back of the shop, which you can visit for a fee.
✉ Passeig de Gràcia 39 ☎ 93 216 01 21 Passeig de Gràcia

ARTS, CRAFTS, GIFTS AND DESIGN

Compagnie Française de l´Orient et de la Chine
Beautiful craft and clothing from the Far East is sold here, from gorgeous ceramics and lacquerware to embroidered slippers and coats and Chairman Mao kitsch. With its wooden shop-fittings and shelves, the shop evokes a colourful colonial market place.
✉ Carrer Valencia 225 ☎ 93 215 48 83 🚇 Passeig de Gràcia

D Barcelona
A wide choice of gifts and avant-garde household items, together with temporary exhibitions presenting the work of talented young designers as well as some of the more established names.
✉ Avinguda Diagonal 367 ☎ 93 216 03 46 🚇 Diagonal

Dom
Homeware, knick-knacks, gadgets and designer toys inspired by the 1960s and 1970s are among the range of goods on sale in this intriguing shop. If it's a beaded curtain or lava lamp you are after, look no further. Books and magazines on art and design are also available.
✉ Carrer Provença 249 ☎ 93 342 55 91 🚇 Diagonal

Dos I Una
The first design shop in Barcelona – it is tiny, but it has a wealth of gadgets and unusual gift ideas including colourful prints and jewellery.
✉ Carrer Rosselló 275 ☎ 93 217 70 32; www.dosiuna.biz 🚇 Diagonal

Puzzlemanía
As the name suggests, Puzzlemanía sells over a thousand different types of jigsaw puzzle.
✉ Carrer Diputació 225 ☎ 93 451 58 03 🚇 Universitat

Vinçon
See page 81.

BOOKS, MUSIC AND ANTIQUES

Casa del Libre

This shop has an enormous selection of books on all subjects and in most languages. Inside the front entrance, coffee-table books on Barcelona are sold, from monographs on Gaudí to Barcelona design tomes.

✉ Passeig de Gràcia 62 ☎ 93 272 34 80 🚇 Passeig de Gràcia

Laie

A very good selection of books, including some foreign titles in a lovely shop with an upstairs cafe which often hosts book readings.

✉ Carrer Pau Claris 85 ☎ 93 318 17 39 ⏰ Cafe: Tue–Fri 8:30am–1am, Sat 10am–1am, Mon 8:30am–9pm 🚇 Urquinaona

FOOD AND DRINK

Cacao Sampaka

This fabulous chocolate "boutique" arranges its chocolate blocks and bon-bons into "collections" such as spices, flowers and so on. You can pick and choose your own selection, or sample some of their goodies in the rear cafe.

✉ Carrer Consell de Cent 292 ☎ 93 272 08 33 🚇 Passeig de Gràcia

Colmado Quillez

Barcelona's most famous traditional grocery store, selling an array of tinned foods, preserves, cold meats and wines.

✉ Rambla de Catalunya 63 ☎ 93 215 23 56 🚇 Passeig de Gràcia

Murrià

This *Modernista* store first opened in 1898, and today sells a wide assortment of cheeses, cold meats and other delicacies.

✉ Carrer Roger de Llúria 85 ☎ 93 215 57 89 🚇 Passeig de Gràcia

Xampany

The only shop devoted solely to the sale of cava (sparkling wine). More than 100 varieties to choose from.

✉ Carrer València 200 ☎ 93 453 93 38 🚇 Passeig de Gràcia

ENTERTAINMENT

Dry Martini

Although it's been around only since the 1980s, this classic cocktail bar a evokes genuine speakeasy ambience with its leather sofas, wooden whiskey-lined shelves, low lighting and smooth jazz on the soundtrack. The cocktails, served by attentive white-aproned waiters, are top flight.

✉ Carrer Aribau 86 ☎ 93 217 50 72 ⏰ Daily 🚇 Diagonal

Luz de Gas

This *fin de siècle* music hall has been made over into one of Barcelona's classiest venues, with live music, from salsa to rock, most nights of the week followed by a DJ to the early hours. Dress up and be prepared to queue at the door at weekends.

✉ Carrer Muntaner 246 ☎ 93 209 77 11 ⏰ Daily 🚇 FGC Muntaner

Nick Havanna

This was one of Barcelona's original "design bars" when it opened in the late 1980s. Although the decor has been trumped in other places, it remains a classic of the city's nightlife.

✉ Carrer Rosselló 208 ☎ 93 217 77 32 ⏰ Thu–Sat midnight–6am 🚇 Diagonal

Omm Bar

Sleek cocktail bar in one of the city's coolest hotels. Live DJs and an affluent playboy crowd make this a fun place to people watch. There's a club downstairs (Wed–Sat).

✉ Rosselló 265 ☎ 93 445 40 00; www.hotelomm.es ⏰ Daily from 6pm 🚇 Diagonal

Otto Zutz

One of the most fashionable and liveliest clubs in town, and a *tour de force* of design, with its clever lighting and metal staircases and galleries. The funk, R&B and elegant house music gets louder as the night progresses. Dress smartly and arrive after midnight.

✉ Carrer Lincoln 15 ☎ 93 238 07 22 ⏰ Wed–Sat midnight–5am 🚇 Fontana, Passeig de Gràcia

Montjuïc to Sants

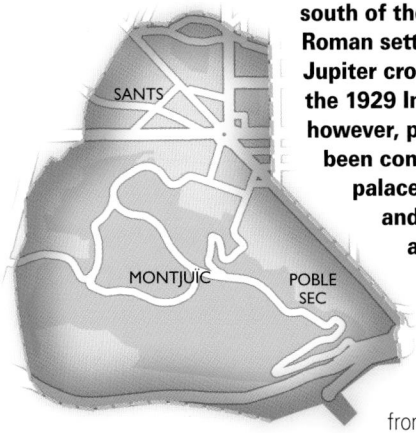

Montjuïc, a steep mountain to the south of the city, once had a Roman settlement and temple to Jupiter crowning its heights. Since the 1929 International Exhibition, however, pretty pavilions have been converted to exhibition palaces, Olympic stadiums and concert halls. There are restaurants here for visitors, but hotels in the area are mainly business-orientated.

Catch the rickety cable car from Barceloneta over the marina and half-way up the hill. From the nearby gondola station (outside the Fundació Joan Miro) glass gondolas offer spectacular views over the city as they whisk you up to the castle. Alternatively, reach the gondola station by the funicular railway, from the Avinguda Paral.lel metro station.

Once on Montjuïc, you'll find two of the city's greatest art museums, one dedicated to Joan Miró and his colourful works, the other showing a world-renowned collection of Catalan Romanesque frescoes rescued from decaying Pyrenean churches.

The Sants neighbourhood, on the northern side of Montjuïc, is where you'll find Barcelona's main train station. At the foot of Montjuïc, on the eastern side, is the residential neighbourhood of Poble Sec with attractive houses and squares, and cafes and bars, particularly along Carrer de Blai.

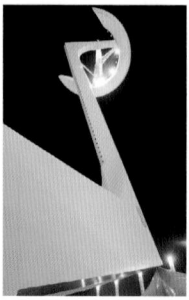

L'ANELLA OLÍMPICA

In 1992, Montjuïc became Barcelona's main venue for the Olympic Games. Atop its western crest lies the Anella Olímpica (Olympic Ring), a vast complex of concrete and marble that contains some of the city's most celebrated new buildings: Ricardo Bofills' neoclassical sports university; the Institut Nacional de Educació Fisica de Catalunya (INEFC); the Complex Esportiu Bernat Picornell swimming-pool complex; Santiago Calatrava's communications tower, which dominates the skyline; and the black steel and glass domed Palau de Sant Jordi, designed by Japanese architect Arata Isozaki

Barcelona had bid for the games three times previously and had built Europe's biggest stadium for the 1929 World Exhibition with the clear intention of using it for the 1936 "People's Olympics" (organized as an alternative to the infamous Berlin Games). These never took place due to the outbreak of Spanish Civil War the day before the official opening. For the 1992 games, local architects preserved the stadium's original facade, while increasing the capacity from 25,000 to 70,000. Highlights of the 1992 games can be relived through video clippings and souvenir showcases in the **Galería Olímpica,** located beneath the stadium.

14K Passeig Olímpic, Montjuïc Palau Sant Jordi: 93 426 20 89; Picornell swimming pools: 93 423 4041 Free (except for events) Espanya, or Paral.lel, then Funicular de Montjuïc 61

Galería Olímpica 93 292 53 79 Mon, Wed–Sat 10–6, Sun 10–2 Moderate 50, 55, 61, PM (Parc Montjüic bus)

CAIXAFORUM

The remodelling of a Puig I Cadafalch Modernist textile factory into an attractive arts centre offers quality free exhibitions and children's entertainment, a good book and gift shop plus a bright, relaxed cafe and restaurant.

www.fundacio.lacaixa.es

15H Avinguda Marquès de Comillas, 6–8 93 476 86 00 Daily 10am–8pm, Sat closes 10pm Cafe-restaurant (€–€€) Espanya 50, 55, 61

FUNDACIÓ JOAN MIRÓ

Best places to see, pages 40–41.

MONTJUÏC

Best places to see, pages 42–43.

MUSEU NACIONAL D'ART DE CATALUNYA

Best places to see, pages 44–45.

PARC DE L'ESPANYA INDUSTRIAL

With works by many Catalan artists, this is Barcelona's most controversial park – a *nou urbanisme* project, built between 1982 and 1985 on the site of an old factory. It is built on two levels, the lower part comprising a large lake and grassy area, with steep white steps up to the much-scorned upper esplanade, where there are ten lighthouses, a series of water spouts and an immense metal play-sculpture entitled the *Dragon of St George*.

15G Carrer de Rector Triado Sants-Estació

PARC DE JOAN MIRÓ

This enduringly popular park occupies an entire city block on what was formerly the site of a massive abattoir, hence its nickname Parc de l'Escorxador (slaughterhouse). It was created in the 1980s, and is always full of people reading, jogging, dog-walking or playing *petanca* (boules)

amid the attractive pergolas and orderly rows of shady palm trees. The park's most famous feature, however, is a startling sculpture 22m (72ft) high by Joan Miró, covered in multicoloured ceramic fragments, named *Dona i Ocell* (Woman and Bird).

16G Carrer de Tarragona Espanya 9, 13, 27, 30, 50, 56, 57, 65, 91, 109, 157

PAVELLÓ MIES VAN DER ROHE

Modernist architect Ludwig Mies van der Rohe created this masterpiece of modern 'international' design for the 1929 World Exhibition at Montjuïc, a construction of astonishing simplicity and finesse in marble, onyx, glass and chrome, widely acknowledged as one of the classic buildings of the 20th century. It was dismantled at the end of the fair and subsequently meticulously reconstructed and reopened (in its original location) in 1986, on the centenary of Mies van der Rohe's birth.

Inside, take time to enjoy the quality of the colours, textures and materials, as well as a striking bronze sculpture entitled *Der Morgen* (The Morning) and the famous Barcelona Chair, a design of timeless elegance, still manufactured today, created by Mies van der Rohe especially for the visit of the King Alphonso XIII of Spain to Expo.

www.miesbcn.com

15J Avinguda del Marquès de Comillas s/n

93 423 40 16 Daily 10–8 Moderate Espanya 13, 50, 61 and all routes to Plaça Espanya

POBLE ESPANYOL

You can tour the whole of Spain in an afternoon here at Barcelona's "Spanish Village", a remarkable showcase of regional architectural styles.

Built for the 1929 World Exhibition, the Poble Espanyol (Spanish Village) was intended as a re-creation of the diversity of Spanish regional architecture through the ages. The 115 life-sized reproductions of buildings, clustered around six squares and 3km (5 miles) of streets, form an authentic village, where visitors can identify famous or characteristic buildings ranging from the patios of Andalucia to Mallorcan mansions and the granite façades of Galicia.

Within the village are bars and restaurants serving regional specialities, and more than 60 shops selling folk crafts and regional artefacts. Some are undeniably over-priced, but there are also some real finds. The Fundació Fran Daural, located inside the 'village', boasts a few Dalís and Picassos and is definitely worth paying the extra, inexpensive entrance fee.

At night the Poble Espanyol takes on a different air with a handful of nightclubs and bars such as La Terrrazza (► 154) and El Tablao de Carmen (► 154) located inside its walls. During the summer during El Grec cultural festival, the main square acts a stage for concerts. In the past years Bob Dylan and Van Morrison have both played here.

www.poble-espanyol.com

15J Avinguda de Marqués de Comillas s/n

93 508 63 00 Mon 9am–8pm; Tue–Thu 9am–2am; Fri–Sat 9am–5am; Sun 9am–11pm Moderate

Plenty (€–€€) Espanya 13, 50, 61

HOTEL

Hotel AC Miramar (€€€)

This luxury hotel is perched on the southern crest of Montjuïc and offers stunning views of the city and sea from its modern rooms.

✉ Plaça Carlos Ibáñez 3 ☎ 93 281 16 00; www.hotelmirarmarbarcelona.es 🚌 50

B (€€)

Overlooking Plaza de Espanya, this modern designer hotel offers stylish accommodation complete with a rooftop terrace and pool.

✉ Gran Via 389 ☎ 93 552 95 00; www.nnhotels.com Espanya

RESTAURANTS

La Parra (€€–€€€)

This former coaching inn is an atmospheric family favourite for simple country cooking – mainly lamb and rabbit roasted over an open fire with *alioli* (garlic mayonnaise) and vegetables accompanied by local wine. There are tables outside in summer.

✉ Carrer de Joanot Matorell 3 ☎ 93 332 51 34 Tue–Sat 8:30am–12:30am, Sun 2–4:30 Hostafrancs

Tapioles 53 (€€)

See page 63.

Xemei (€€)

This pretty restaurant serves excellent Venetian food such as spaghetti with clams and rice cooked in squid ink.

✉ Passeig de l'Exposició 85 ☎ 93 553 51 40 Thu–Mon Poble Sec

TAPAS BARS

Mirador

With one of the best views in town this large outside terrace next to where the cable car arrives from Barceloneta is a great place for a break. Sit back in the sun with a drink in your hand and gaze at the city and the coast spread out below you.

✉ Carretera Miramar, Montjuïc Daily 10–7

Quimet i Quimet
See page 61.

SHOPPING

Gallery gift shops
The excellent gift shops at the Fundació Joan Miró (➤ 40–41), at MNAC (➤ 44–45) and at La CaixaFòrum (➤ 149) offer a great mix of good-value souvenirs and presents to take home. Great places to browse.

Poble Espanyol
A collection of more than 60 art and craft shops in a showcase reproduction "Spanish Village" (➤ 152) selling traditional wares from all corners of Spain. Plenty of bars and restaurants here as well.
✉ Avinguda del Marqués de Comillas s/n ☎ 93 508 63 00 🚌 13, 61
🚇 Espanya

ENTERTAINMENT

Space
This smaller version of the famous Ibizan club packs them in at weekends. Popular with a mainly young crowd of techno and house enthusiasts.
✉ Carrer Tarragona 141–147 ☎ 93 426 84 44 🕐 Fri–Sat midnight–6am
🚇 Tarragona

El Tablao de Carmen
Highly rated flamenco cabaret at the Poble Espanyol. Dinner is also available.
✉ Carrer Arcs 9, Poble Espanyol, Montjuïc ☎ 93 325 68 95 🕐 Tue–Sun 8pm–2am ❓ Shows Tue–Sun 9:30 and 11:30pm. Reservations recommended

La Terrrazza
Summertime open-air club takes place on Montjüic, behind Poble Espanyol.
✉ Avinguda MArquès de Comilas, Montjüic ☎ 93 272 49 80; www.laterrrazza.com

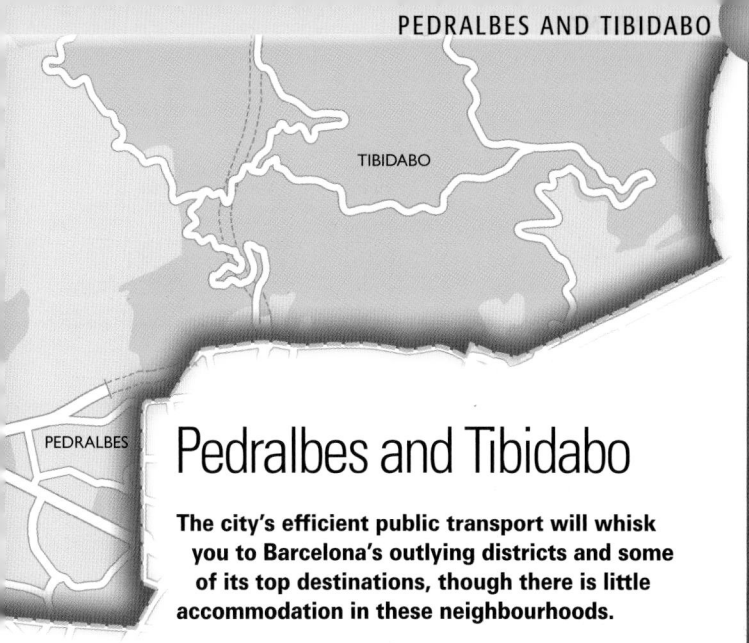

Pedralbes and Tibidabo

The city's efficient public transport will whisk you to Barcelona's outlying districts and some of its top destinations, though there is little accommodation in these neighbourhoods.

In the western neighbourhood of Pedralbes sits the splendid royal monastery of the same name, the perfect place to escape the bustle of the city. South of the monastery, off the Avinguda Diagonal, lies the Palau Reial de Pedralbes, a royal palace that now houses a museum of ceramics and a museum of decorative arts. The section of the Avinguda Diagonal that cuts through the district of Les Corts, between the Palau Reial de Pedralbes and Plaça de Francesc Macià, is lined with offices, banks and apartment buildings, though a mega-mall and classy shops make it a popular place for retail therapy.

To the south is FC Barcelona's stadium, Camp Nou, where football fans flock to see their team in action. To the north is Tibidabo, where you can ride on roller-coasters with the whole city laid out spectacularly before you.

CAMP NOU AND MUSEU DEL FUTBOL CLUB BARCELONA

Even those who loathe football can't help marvelling at the vast Camp Nou stadium, which seats more than 98,000 spectators. If you can't get a ticket to see one of Europe's top football teams in action, then at least visit the Barcelona Football Club Museum, the city's most visited museum after the Picasso Museum (➤ 46–47). The extensive tour includes the visitor's changing rooms, the press and royal boxes as well as an emotional entrance onto the ground through the tunnel. The museum, under the terraces, presents a triumphant array of trophies, photographs and replays of highlights in the club's history before leading you to the shop, where everyone can buy that essential club shirt, scarf, badge...

FC Barcelona, or Barça for short, is more than a football club. During the Franco era, it stood as a Catalan symbol around which people could rally, and this emotional identification still remains today. It also explains why this legendary club has the world's largest soccer club membership (more than 140,000 members) and why the streets still erupt with ecstatic revellers following a win over arch-rivals, Real Madrid.

www.fcbarcelona.com

1D ✉ Camp Nou – Entrance 7 or 9, Carrer Arístides Maillol
☎ 93 496 36 00 Mon–Sat 10–8, Sun 10–2:30 Expensive Cafe (€)
Collblanc, Palau Real 7, 33, 60, 63, 67, 74, 75, 113 Gift shop

MONESTIR DE PEDRALBES

The monastery of Pedralbes was founded by King Jaume II and Queen Elisenda de Montcada in 1326 to accommodate nuns of the St Clare of Assisi order. Following the king's death in 1327, Elisenda spent the last 37 years of her life here.

The spacious, three-storey cloisters are one of the architectural jewels of Barcelona. Step inside and it is hard to believe you are just a short bus ride from downtown Barcelona. From here, there is access to the refectory, the chapter house and the queen's grave. St Michael's Chapel is one of the highlights of a visit. It is decorated with remarkable murals by Spanish painter Ferrer Bassa depicting Christ's Passion and the life of the Virgin Mary.

Monastic life in the 14th century is illustrated through permanent exhibitions in the original refectory, with its vaulted ceiling, the infirmary and the kitchens. Next door in the Gothic church you can hear nuns of the founding order sing during Mass.

2A Baixada de Monestir 9 93 256 34 34 Monastery: Tue–Sun 10–2. Church: Tue–Sun 11–2, 6:30–8. Daily Mass at 7pm Moderate 22, 63, 64, 75 Bookshop, gift shop

PALAU REIAL DE PEDRALBES

The Royal Palace of Pedralbes accommodated the Spanish Royal family during the International Exhibition of 1929. After 1939 it was used by Franco and then royalty and heads of state, before being opened to the public in 1960, along with the stately gardens. Today the state rooms house major museums. The Museu de Ceràmica traces the development of Spanish ceramics from the 12th century onwards, and includes the 18th-century Catalan panels *La Cursa de Braus* (the Bullfight) and *La Xocolotada* (The Chocolate Party), together with works by Picasso and Miró.

The two separate collections of the Disseny Hub are housed in the palace while a new home is built for them. The Museu Tèxtil i d'Indumentària is a costume collection displayed in chronological order with a handful of beautiful creations from Cristóbal Balenciega from the 1950s. The Museu de les Arts Decoratives has an impressive collection of furniture and design from the early Middle Ages to the present day with special emphasis placed on 20th-century developments.

www.museuceramica.bcn.es

www.dhub-bcn.cat

2C Avinguda de la Diagonal 686 93 256 34 65 Museums: Tue–Sun 10–6. Park: open until dusk Museums: inexpensive, free Sun after 3pm and 1st Sun of month Palau Reial 7, 33, 60, 63, 67, 74, 75, 113 Shop, library

TIBIDABO AND SERRA DE COLLSEROLA

Mont Tibidabo, 550m (1,800ft) high, forms the northwestern boundary of Barcelona and has panoramic views over the entire city, and, on exceptionally clear days, of Mallorca. The best views are from the **Torre de Collserola,** a telecommunications tower with a lookout point. At its summit, and topped by a huge statue of Christ, stands the modern Church of the Sacred Heart (Sagrat Cor). Near by, the **Parc d'Atraccions** (► 69) cleverly balances traditional rides with high-tech attractions on several levels of the mountaintop, and is a fun day out for the family. Tibidabo is just one of the mountains of the Collserola range, a wonderful 6,550ha (16,200-arce) nature reserve with woodlands full of wildlife. It is best reached by FGC train to Baixador de Vallvidrera. From here, it is a 10-minute walk uphill to the **information centre,** where details of walks and cycles are available.

7A (off map)

Tibidabo Amusement Park

Plaça Tibidabo 3–4 93 221 79 42; www.tibidabo.es Jul–Aug Wed–Sun noon–11. Check website for other dates Expensive FGC Avinguda Tibidabo, then Tramvia Blau to Peu Funicular, then funicular

Torre de Collserola

Carretera de Vallvidrera al Tibidabo s/n 93 406 93 54; www.torredecollserola.com Mon–Fri 11–2:30, 3:30–6, Sat–Sun 11–6; closes 2 hours later Jul, Aug Moderate FGC Peu Funicular, then funicular

Collserola Information Centre

Carretera de Vallvidrera a Sant Cugat, al km 4.7 93 280 35 52; www.parccollserola.net Daily 9:30–3 FGC Baixador de Vallvidrera, then 10-minute walk

HOTEL

Gran Hotel La Florida (€€€)

Located 500m (1,640ft) above the city, this hotel has superb views of Barcelona and the Mediterranean and offers luxurious accommodation. There is original art work in the public spaces and an L-shaped lap pool on a superb terrace.

✉ Carretera de Vallvidrera al Tibidabo 83–93 ☎ 93 259 30 00; www.hotellaflorida.com

RESTAURANTS

Fragments (€)

This charming cafe on the prettiest square in Les Corts offers excellent tapas in the front room and more substantial meals in the dining room and garden. The *patatas bravas* (fried potatoes in a spicy sauce) are memorable, and it serves a great value *menu del día*.

✉ Plaça de la Concòrdia 12 ☎ 93 419 96 13 ⏰ Wed–Sun
🚇 Les Corts

La Venta (€€)

At the very foot of the funicular up to Tibidabo this pretty flower-decked restaurant has tables both in the *Modernista* dining rooms and outside. The good Mediterranean food ranges from traditional to innovative.

✉ Plaça sel Dr Andreu ☎ 93 212 64 55 ⏰ Mon–Sat 🚇 FGC Avinguda Tibidabo

SHOPPING

L'Illa

L'Illa is a large shopping mall full of national and international chain stores offering the latest in fashion, jewellery and homeware. There is a particularly good food hall in the basement where you can buy to take home or pull up a chair at one of the quality outlets and enjoy dishes ranging from fresh seafood and sushi to pasta and Spanish classics.

✉ Avinguda Diagonal 557 ☎ 93 444 00 00; www.lilla.com ⏰ Mon–Sat 9:30am–9:30pm 🚇 Maria Cristina

ENTERTAINMENT

Bikini

One of Barcelona's best nightspots, with a club playing rock/disco, a Latin-American salsa room and a classy cocktail lounge.

✉ Carrer Deu i Mata 105 ☎ 93 322 00 05 ⏲ Wed–Sun midnight–5am 🚇 Les Corts

Danzatoria

With its restaurant, disco, terrace café and rambling gardens on the slopes of Tibidabo, this sophisticated place is a favourite summer venue, despite the lengthy uphill trek from the station.

✉ Avinguda Tibidabo 61 ☎ 93 221 62 61 ⏲ Daily 10pm–3am 🚇 FGC Avinguda Tibidabo

Elephant

Glamorous bar-club in a Modernista building complete with a tower. The decor is Persian palace meets Indian temple; the music is a happy mixture of mainstream pop, dance and chill out.

✉ Passeig dels Til·lers 1 ☎ 93 334 02 58 ⏲ Wed–Sat 11:30pm–4am 🚇 Palau Reial

Mirablau (€)

There are few more spectacular places in Barcelona than Mirablau where you can sip a cocktail and drink in the breathtaking views of the whole city from this hillside bar. Snacks are available during the day and a nightclub downstairs opens at 11pm. The prices are high but it's worth a splurge.

✉ Plaça Doctor Andreu 2 ☎ 93 418 58 79; www.mirablaubcn.com ⏲ Mon–Fri 11–4:30am, Sat, Sun 11–5am 🚇 Tramvia Blau

Sala BeCool

Live indie music and a late-night club that pulls in, as the name says, a cool crowd, with concerts, live acts and DJ sessions featuring local, national and international artists.

✉ Plaça Joan Llongueras 5 ☎ 93 362 04 13; www.salabecool.com ⏲ Club sessions: Thu–Sat midnight–3am. Live gigs generally start 9–10pm 🚇 FGC Muntaner

Excursions

Figueres	165
Girona	166–167
Montserrat	168–169
El Penedès	170–173
Sitges	174–175
Tarragona	176–179

It would be a shame to visit Barcelona without also seeing something of Catalunya (Catalonia). Despite being an autonomous province of Spain, this region feels in many ways like a separate country, with its own language and traditions, culture and cuisine. Its geographical location makes it the gateway to Spain. Over time the passage of many peoples and civilizations has shaped the region, leaving cities such as Girona and Tarragona brimming with historical monuments, while its beautiful landscapes have provided inspiration for such artists as Gaudí, Miró, Dalí and Picasso.

The Catalan landscape is easy to tour and offers a wide variety of scenery, from the dramatic, snow-capped peaks of the Pyrenees and the secret bays and bustling fishing ports of the Costa Brava, north of Barcelona, to the acclaimed Penedès vineyards and long golden beaches of the Costa Daurada to the south.

FIGUERES

The main claim to fame of Figueres, two hours' drive northwest of Barcelona and 17km (10.5 miles) from the Franco-Spanish border, is that the great Surrealist painter Salvador Dalí was born here in 1904 and gave his first exhibition here when he was just 14. In 1974, he inaugurated his **Teatre-Museu Dalí**, in the old municipal theatre, and it remains one of Spain's most visited museums. It is the only museum in Europe dedicated exclusively to his works.

The building, topped with a massive metallic dome and decorated with egg shapes, is original and spectacular – in keeping with Dalí's powerful personality. Its galleries are housed in a number of enclosed, circular tiers around a central stage and a courtyard containing a "Rainy Cadillac" and a tower of car tyres crowned by a boat and an umbrella. The galleries contain paintings, sculptures, jewellery, drawings and other works from his private collection along with weird and wonderful constructions from different periods of his career, including a bed with fish tails, skeletal figures and even a complete life-sized orchestra. Dalí died in Figueres in 1989, leaving his entire estate to the Spanish State. His body lies behind a simple granite slab inside the museum.

Plaça del Sol, 972 50 31 55

Teatre-Museu Dalí

Plaça Gala-Salvador Dalí 5 ☎ 972 67 75 00; www.salvador-dali.org

Jul–Sep daily 9–8; Oct, Mar–Jun Tue–Sun 9:30–6; Nov–Feb Tue–Sun 10:30–6 Expensive Last ticket sold 45 minutes before closing

GIRONA

Just 1.5 hours by car or train from Barcelona, the beautiful, walled city of Girona is one of Catalonia's most characterful cities, with an admirable collection of ancient monuments. The old city, built on a steep hill and known for its lovely stairways, arcaded streets and sunless alleys, is separated from modern Girona by the River Onyar. The medieval, multicoloured houses overhanging the river are a photographer's dream, especially when seen from the iron footbridge designed by Eiffel. Most of the main sights are in the old city. Make sure you also allow time to shop along the beautiful Rambla de la Llibertat and to enjoy a drink in the arcaded Plaça de la Independencia.

At the heart of the old city, centred around Carrer de la Força, El Call, the old Jewish quarter, is one of the best preserved in western Europe and is particularly atmospheric by night, with its street lanterns and intimate restaurants. Another splendid sight is the **Catedral**, with its impressive staircase leading up to a fine baroque facade, a magnificent medieval interior and the widest Gothic vault in Europe. Housed inside a monastery, the **Museu Arqueològic** (Archaeological Musuem) outlines the city's history, and provides access to the Passeig Arqueològic, a panoramic walk around the walls of the old city. Near by, the 12th-century **Banys Arabs** (Arab Bathhouse), probably designed by Moorish craftsmen following the Moors' occupation of Girona, is the best preserved of its kind in Spain after the Alhambra, and is particularly striking for its fusion of Arab and Romanesque styles.

Rambla de la Llibertat 1, 972 22 65 75; www.girona.cat/turisme

Catedral

Plaça de la Catedral 972 21 44 26; www.catedraldegirona.org Daily 10–7 Moderate; free Sat pm and Sun

Museu Arqueològic

Monestir Sant Pere de Galligans 972 20 26 32 Jun–Sep Tue–Sat 10:30–1:30, 4–7, Sun 10–2:30; Oct–May Tue–Sat 10–2, 4–6, Sun 10–2:30 Inexpensive

Banys Arabs

Carrer Ferran Catolic 972 19 07 97; www.banysarabs.org Apr–Sep Mon–Sat 10–7, Sun 10–2; Oct–Mar daily 10–2 Inexpensive

MONTSERRAT

Catalonia's holy mountain is 56km (35 miles) northwest of Barcelona with a summit of 1,200m (3,937ft) reached by a cable-car ride or a rack railway. Montserrat is named after its serrated rock formations (*mont*, mountain; *serrat*, sawed) and is one of the most important pilgrimage sites in Spain. Thousands travel here every year to venerate a medieval statue of the Madonna and Child called *La Moreneta* (The Black Virgin). The statue is said to have been made by St Luke around AD50 and brought to the area by St Peter, and is displayed above the altar of the monastery church.

The spectacularly located monastery, founded in 1025, is also famous for its choir, *La Escolania*, one of the oldest and best-known boys' choirs in Europe, dating from the 13th century. The choir sings daily in the **Basilica,** a striking edifice containing important paintings including works by El Greco and Caravaggio.

There are splendid walks to be had in the hillside above the monastery (reached by a short funicular ride). Many of the routes have been paved and most graded, some of the most popular are to the ancient hermitages.

Plaça de la Creu, Montserrat, 93 877 77 77; www.abadiamontserrat.net

Limited choice of bars and restaurants

Basilica

Monestir de Montserrat Daily 8–6:30. La Escolania performs Mon–Fri at 1pm, Mon–Thu at 6:45pm, Sun at noon FGC line R5 from Plaça d'Espanya to Aeri de Montserrat (for cable car); or Monistrol (for rack railway or *cremellera*; www.cremalleradeMontserrat.com)

EL PENEDÈS

Just an hour by train from Barcelona, El Penedès is Catalonia's wine country, perhaps not as well known outside Spain as La Rioja but producing some excellent wines all the same. Many *bodegas* (wineries) are open to the public (► 172). But even if you are not particularly interested in viniculture, El Penedès is a glorious place to visit, with its valleys of vineyards, pretty medieval villages and proximity to Montserrat (► 169), Catalonia's "sacred mountain".

The capital of the region is the bustling Vilafranca, a handsome town with some pretty *Modernista* architecture and arcaded streets in the old quarter. In the Gothic quarter, surrounded by squares, palaces and churches, the **Museu de les Cultures del Vi de Catalunya** is the only museum in Catalonia to be wholly dedicated to wine. Current methods of production can be observed at Vilafranca's three top wineries – **Mas Tinell, Jean León** and **Miguel Torres** – all outside the town centre (ask at the tourist office (► 172) for details. Every Saturday morning a produce market is held in Plaça de la Vila in front of the Gothic *ajuntament* (town hall). Farmers come from all over the region to set up stalls, and it's a great place to pick up olives, charcuterie, cheeses and other local delicacies. While you are here, visit the Basílica de Santa Maria in the adjacent Plaça Sant Jaume (contact tourist office for opening hours), a 15th-century Gothic church and climb the 52m (170ft) bell tower for a great view of Vilafranca's interesting skyline. Vilafranca is famous for its *castellers* (human towers that perform during the city's main *festa*, held during the last week of August) and opposite the church a monument has been erected in their honour. Off and around the square the narrow streets are full of good bars, serving local wines and dishes such as *xató*, an endive and cod salad served with a delicious sauce of nuts, olive oil and dried peppers.

The villages around Vilafranca are definitely worth exploring. Sant Marti Sarroca contains an important Romanesque church with a splendid Gothic altarpiece and a 9th-century castle. Sant Sadorni d'Anoia is where most of El Penedès' cava (local sparkling wine) is produced with

66 cava firms dotted throughout the town. The largest, Codorníu, produces around 40 million bottles a year and its magnificent *Modernista* plant is open to visitors daily. Tours last 90 minutes and include a tasting. In Freixenet, the village's most emblematic *bodega,* built in *Modernista* style, is located right next to its railway station. In Torrelles de Foix, panoramic views of the entire area can be had from the Sanctuario de la Virgen de Foix, an ancient church built in honour of the region's patron saint. The village is also famous for Fuentes de les Dous, 35 natural springs that form a pretty waterfall.

The best time to visit El Penedès is in September during harvest when the **vineyards** are a hive of activity. Many villages also hold *verema* festivals, when the first wines of the season are drunk, usually in early October. Dates vary so check at the tourist office for details.

Vilafranca de Penedès Tourist Office

✉ Carrer de la Fruita 13, 93 818 12 54

Museu de les Cultures del Vi de Catalunya

✉ Plaça Jaume I, 1 and 3, Vilafranca del Penedès ☎ 93 890 05 82; www.museosdelvino.es ⏲ Jun–Aug Tue–Sat 10–7, Sun 10–2; Sep–May Tue–Sat 10–2, 4–7, Sun 10–2 ✋ Inexpensive

Penedès Wineries

Codorníu ☎ 93 891 33 42; www.codorniu.es
Jean León ☎ 93 899 55 12; www.jeanleon.com
Mas Tinell ☎ 93 817 05 86; www.mastinell.com
Miguel Torres ☎ 93 817 74 00; www.torres.es
Freixenet ☎ 93 891 70 00; www.freixenet.es
⏲ Opening times vary. Contact individual wineries for details

2

SITGES

Sitges, 40km (25 miles) south of Barcelona, is one of Spain's oldest bathing resorts and has long been the weekend and holiday playground of Barcelonans. It was once a sleepy fishing port and, although it has now developed into a thriving seaside destination, the old town still retains its ancient charm, with narrow streets, whitewashed cottages and flower-festooned balconies. It also has several appealing *Modernista* buildings.

It was artist and writer Santiago Rusinyol who first put Sitges on the map, bringing it to the attention of artists such as Manuel de Falla, Ramon Casas, Nonell, Utrillo and Picasso. Rusinyol's house, **Cau Ferrat**, is today a museum, containing works by El Greco and Picasso among others. Neighbouring **Museu Maricel de Mar** houses an interesting collection of medieval and baroque artefacts, and the nearby **Museu Romántic** provides a fascinating insight into 18th-century patrician life in Sitges.

Sitges is famous for its beautiful Platja d'Or (Golden Beach), which stretches southwards for 5km (3 miles) from the baroque church of Sant Bartomeu i Santa Tecla. Its palm-fringed promenade is dotted with beach bars, cafes and fish restaurants. However, the resort is perhaps best known for its vibrant nightlife, drawing a young cosmopolitan crowd throughout the summer season. It is also a popular gay holiday destination. From October to May, Sitges is considerably quieter, except during *Carnaval* in mid-February when the town once more comes alive with wild parties and showy parades, drawing spectators from afar.

Carrer Sinia Morera 1, 93 894 42 51; www.sitgestour.com

Museums

Cau Ferrat and Maricel de Mar: Carrer Fonolar; Romántic: Casa Llopis, Carrer Sant Gaudenci 1 Cau Ferrat and Maricel de Mar: 93 894 03 64; Romántic: 93 894 29 69 Jul–Sep Tue–Sat 9:30–2, 4–7, Sun 10–3; Oct–Jun Tue–Sat 9:30–2, 3:30–6:30, Sun 10–3 Cau Ferrat: moderate. Maricel de Mar and Romántic: inexpensive. Combined ticket available for all three museums Guided visits only, on the hour

TARRAGONA

This agreeable city is not very well known to most foreign visitors to the region, even though it contains the largest example of Roman remains in Spain, the remarkable architectural legacy of Roman Tarraco, and was once capital of an area that covered half the Iberian peninsula. Originally settled by Iberians and then Carthaginians, it later became the base for the Roman conquest of Spain and the main commercial centre on this stretch of the coast until Barcelona and Valencia overshadowed it, after the Christian reconquest of Spain in the early 12th century.

The town is situated on a rocky hill, sloping down to the sea. The ancient upper town contains most of the Roman ruins, some interesting museums and an attractive medieval quarter with a grand cathedral. Below the Old Town lies the modern shopping district, centred on the Rambla Nova with its smart boutiques and restaurants, and a daily fruit and vegetable market in Plaça Corsini. Below the main town, the chief attraction of the lower part of the city is the maritime district of El Serrallo with its colourful fishing fleet, traditional *Lonja* (fish auction), and dockside restaurants. The rocky coastline beyond conceals a couple of beaches, notably Platja Arrabassada and Platja Llarga.

In the hillside overlooking the sea, the **Amfiteatre Romà** (Roman Amphitheatre) was where the Romans held their public spectacles, including combats between gladiators and wild animals before an audience of 12,000 people. During the 12th century the

Romanesque church of Santa Maria del Miracle was built on the site, giving the beach below its name – El Miracle. Tarragona's grandiose **Catedral** – a magnificent Romanesque-Gothic building – was built as the centrepiece of the *ciutat antigua* (old city).

The fascinating **Museu Arqueològic** (Archaeological Museum) includes a section of the old Roman wall, statues of emperors, several sarcophagi and some interesting mosaics. Near by stands

the Praetorium and the vaults of the first-century Roman Circus. The Praetorium is the site of the **Museu d'Història** (Tarragona History Museum), which traces the origins and history of the city through such treasures as the sarcophagus of Hipolitus, a masterpiece that was rescued from the sea in 1948.

Tarragona's most treasured Roman remains are housed in the **Museu i Necropolia Paleocristians** (Paleo-Christian Museum), in what was once an ancient necropolis, a 20-minute walk west of the city centre. It includes a valuable collection of mosaics, pottery, metalwork, glass and ivory.

For an overview of the old city and the hinterland of the Camp de Tarragona, walk the Passeig Arqueològic. This promenade encircles the northernmost half of the old town, around the Roman walls, of which 1km (0.5 miles) of the original 4km (2.5 miles) remains. Seven of the original defence towers and gates still stand.

Carrer Major 3a, 977 25 07 95 You can visit the Amfiteatre, Passeig Arqueològic, Museu d'Història, Circ Romà and Casa Museu de Castellarnau on a combined ticket

Amfiteatre Romà

Carrer Oleguer 977 24 25 79 Apr–Sep Tue–Sat 9–9, Sun 9–3; Oct–Mar Tue–Sat 9–3, Sun 10–3 Inexpensive

Catedral

Plaça de la Seu 977 23 86 85 Jun to mid-Oct Mon–Sat 10–1, 4–7; mid-Oct to mid-Mar Mon–Sat 10–5; mid-Mar to May Mon–Sat 10–6

Museu Arqueològic

Plaça del Rei 5 977 23 62 09 Jun–Sep Tue–Sat 9:30–8:30, Sun 10–2; Oct–May Tue–Sat 9:30–6, Sun 10–2 Inexpensive

Museu de Història

Plaça del Rei 977 24 22 20 Apr–Sep Tue–Sat 9–9, Sun 9–3; Oct–Mar Tue–Sat 9–7, Sun 10–3 Moderate

Museu i Necropolia Paleocristians

Aviguda Ramón y Cajal 977 23 62 09 Mar–May, Oct 9:30–1:30, 3–6; Nov–Feb 9:30–1:30, 3–5:30; Jun–Sep 10–1:30, 4–8

HOTELS

FIGUERES

Hotel Durán (€)

This smart, attractive hotel also has a highly regarded restaurant that serves hearty traditional cuisine with a modern touch. It was a favourite haunt of Salvador Dalí and friends.

✉ Carrer Lasuaca 5 ☎ 972 50 12 50; www.hotelduran.com

GIRONA

Bellmirall (€)

Housed inside the ancient buildings of the Jewish quarter and near to the cathedral, this friendly 1-star hotel feels more like a country dwelling – and it serves huge breakfasts to keep you going through the day.

✉ Carrer Bellmirall 3 ☎ 972 20 40 09; www.grn.es/bellmirall

Hotel Llegendes De Girona Cathedral (€€)

Swish contemporary hotel in an ancient building with fabulous cathedral views from many of the attractive ensuite bedrooms.

✉ Portal de la Barca 4 ☎ 972 22 09 05; www.hotel-llegendes.com

MONTSERRAT

Abat Cisneros (€)

The name of this 3-star hotel, set in Montserrat's main square, is derived from a title given to the head of Benedictine monasteries during the Middle Ages. Some of the hotel's plain rooms are near the monastery and others are in the former monks' cells.

✉ Plaça de Monestir, 08199 Montserrat ☎ 93 877 77 01; www.montserratvisita.com

SITGES

Hotel Calipolis (€€)

A big, bright hotel right on the seafront offering newly refurbished rooms most with stunning sea views and private balconies. The swimming pool and rooftop sundeck are the stars of the many facilities.

✉ Avinguda de Sofía 2–6 ☎ 938 941 500; www.hotelcalipolis.com

El Xalet (€)
El Xalet is a discreet hotel in a beautiful *Modernista* villa, with just 11 well-furnished rooms. Other facilities include a restaurant, swimming pool and garden.
✉ Carrer Isla de Cuba 35 ☎ 93 811 00 70; www.elxalet.com

TARRAGONA

Imperial Tarraco (€€)
The Imperial Tarraco is currently Tarragona's top hotel (4-star). It is centrally situated overlooking both the sea and the Amfiteatre Romà (► 176).
✉ Passeig de Palmeres ☎ 977 23 30 40; www.husa.es

Hotel Lauria (€)
An impressive building houses this well-located hotel, close to shops and restaurants, with pleasant functional rooms and a small outdoor pool.
✉ Rambla Nova ☎ 20 977 236 712; www.hlauria.es

Hotel Plaça de la Font (€)
A cosy, unpretentious hotel in the very heart of the old town offering 20 plain, ensuite rooms.
✉ Plaça de la Font ☎ 26 97 724 61 34; www.hotelpdelafont.com

RESTAURANTS

GIRONA

Blanc (€€)
Just across the river from the old town, this stylish white restaurant presents carefully designed plates of Mediterranean food at good prices.
✉ Nord 2 ☎ 97 241 56 37; www.blanc-restaurant.com ⏲ Daily

Zanpanzar (€–€€)
A small Basque tapas bar with an attached restaurant and outside tables serving top-notch *pintxos* (Basque-style tapas), which are displayed across the bar.
✉ Carrer Cort Reial 10–12 ☎ 97 221 28 43 ⏲ Tue–Sun

MONTSERRAT

Abat Cisneros (€€–€€€)

Montserrat's top restaurant. The 16th-century stone dining room used to contain the monastery stables.

✉ Hotel Abat Cisneros ☎ 93 877 77 01 ⏲ Daily

SITGES

El Celler Vell (€€)

Just off the main drag in the old town, Carrer Sant Francesc, this rustic wine bar serves up a selection of home-made Catalan specialities. Try the tasty salads or the traditional fish dishes like hake *suquet* with prawns.

✉ Sant Bonaventura 21 ☎ 93 811 19 61 ⏲ Closed Wed and lunch Mon, Tue, Thu

Mare Nostrum (€€)

Smart waterfront restaurant. Try the *Xato de Sitges* (grilled fish with a local variant of *romesco* sauce), or monkfish and prawns with garlic mousseline.

✉ Passeig de la Ribera 60–62 ☎ 93 894 33 93 ⏲ Closed Wed and mid-Dec to Jan

TARRAGONA

Bodega Celler Gras (€)

A good place to join the locals for tapas – pâtés, cheeses and charcuterie, including spicy *xoriço* and Mallorquin *sobrassada*.

✉ Carrer Governadir Gonzalez 8 ☎ 977 23 48 20 ⏲ Daily, closed Sun pm

Estació Maritima (€€€)

This is one of the best of the many fish restaurants and tapas bars that line the waterfront in the fishermen's district of Serralló.

✉ Moll de Costa Tinglade 4 ☎ 977 22 74 18 ⏲ Closed Mon, Sun pm

Sol-Ric (€€)

Excellent fish restaurant located in an old *masia* (country house) on the outskirts of town towards Platja Rembassada.

✉ Via Augusta 227 ☎ 977 23 20 32 ⏲ Closed Sun, Mon pm

Sight Locator Index

This index relates to the maps on the covers. We have given map references to the main sights in the book. Some sights may not be plotted on the maps.

L'Anella Olímpica **14K**
La Barceloneta **21L**
Barri Gòtic **20K or *3c***
CaixaForum **15H**
Camp Nou and Museu del Futbol Club Barcelona **1D**
Casa Asia **8F**
Casa Milà (La Pedrera) **8F**
Catedral ***4c***
Disseny Hub Montcada **21K**
Drassanes Reials and Museu Marítim **19L**
L'Eixample **19G**
Fundació Antoni Tàpies **20G**
Fundacío Joan Miró **16K**
Gràcia **9E**
Hospital de la Santa Creu i Sant Pau **12E**
Manzana de la Discordia **20G**
Mercat de la Boqueria **19J or *1b***
Monestir de Pedralbes **2A**
Montjuïc **16K**
Monument a Colom **19L or *1f***
Museu d'Art Contemporani de Barcelona (MABCA) **19J**
Museu Egipci de Barcelona **20G**
Museu Frederic Marès **20K or *4c***
Museu d'Història de Catalunya **21L**
Museu d'Història de la Ciutat **20K or *4c***
Museu Nacional d'Art de Catalunya (MNAC) **15J**
Museu Picasso **21K**
Museu Tèxtil i d'Indumentària **21K**
Palau Güell **19K or *1d***
Palau de la Música Catalana **21J**
Palau Reial de Pedralbes **2C**
Parc de la Ciutadella **22K**
Parc de la Creueta del Coll **10B**
Parc de l'Espanya Industrial **15G**
Parc de Joan Miró **16G**
Park Güell **10C**
Pavelló Mies van der Rohe **15J**
Plaça de Catalunya **20H**
Plaça del Rei **20K or *4c***
Plaça Reial **19K or *2d***
Plaça Sant Jaume **20K or *3c***
Les Platjas **21M**
Poble Espanyol **15J**
Port Olímpic **23M**
Port Vell **20L**
Las Ramblas **19K or *1d***
La Sagrada Família **23G**
Santa Maria del Mar **21K**
Tibidabo and Serra de Collserola **7A (off map)**
Torre Agbar **24H (off map)**

Index

accommodation 101–102, 121, 139, 153, 160, 180–181
air travel 26
airport and air travel 26
Amfiteatre Romà 176, 179
L'Anella Olímpica 148–149
antiques 110, 145
L'Aquàrium 68, 100
Arab Bath-house 166, 167
arts, crafts, gifts and design 109–110, 144, 154

banks 30, 32
Banys Arabs 166, 167
Barcelona Football Club Museum 68, 156
Barcelona Museum of Contemporary Art 92–93
La Barceloneta 114–115
Barri Gòtic 16, 72–73, 85, 86–88
bars 111–112, 126, 146, 154, 161
beaches 68, 114–115
bicycle tours 71
boat trips 27
book and music shops 110–111, 145
Bus Turístic 11, 27
buses 11, 27, 70

cable cars 28, 68
cafes 58–59, 106–107, 123–124, 142
CaixaForum 68, 149
El Call (Girona) 166
Camp Nou 68, 156, 157, 161
Canon's House 72
car rental 28
Casa Amatller 134
Casa Asia 128
Casa Batlló 134–135
Casa del Cánonges 72
Casa de la Ciutat 99
Casa Lleó-Morera 135
Casa Milà (La Pedrera) 16, 36–37
Casa-Museu Gaudí 49
Casa Padellàs 94
Casa Vicens 131
Catalunya (Catalonia) 11, 164–183
Catedral, Barcelona 38–39
Catedral, Girona 166, 167
Catedral, Tarragona 178, 179
Cau Ferrat 175
children's attractions 68–69
City History Museum 94
Ciutadella Park 74, 120
Ciutat Vella 87
climate 22
concessions 28–29
credit cards 30
crime and personal safety 32
currency and foreign exchange 30

Dalí, Salvador 16, 165
dental services 23
Disseny Hub Montcada (DHUB) 116
Drassanes Reials 88–89
drink driving 28
drinking water 31
driving 22, 27, 28
drugs and medicines 31

eating out 58–59, 60–61, 62–63, 103–107, 121–124, 140–142, 153, 160, 181–182
economy 11
Egyptian Museum of Barcelona 137
L'Eixample 10, 19, 127, 129
electricity 32
embassies and consulates 31
emergency telephone numbers 31
entertainment 111–112, 126, 146, 154, 161
Església dels Sants Just i Pastor 73

fares 28–29
fashion shopping 19, 107–108, 124–125, 142–143
FC Barcelona 19, 68, 156
festivals and events 24–25
Figueres 165
flamenco 154
Font Monumental 120
food and drink 12–15, 110, 125, 145 *see also* eating out
football 19, 68, 156
fuel 28
Fundació Antoni Tàpies 130
Fundació Fran Daural 152
Fundació Joan Miró 40–41
funiculars 28

Galería Olímpica 149
gardens 74–75
Gaudí, Antoni 16, 36, 48–49, 52–53, 85, 95, 98, 134
General Library of Art History 45
geography 11
Girona 166–167
golondrinas 27, 68, 71, 100
Gothic Quarter 16, 72–73, 85, 86–88
Gràcia 127, 131
Great Royal Palace 97

health advice 22, 23, 31
Hospital de la Santa Creu i Sant Pau 132

IMAX Cinema 100
insurance 22, 23
internet services 30

Jardí Botànic 74

King's Square 97

language 33

Magic Fountain 43
Manzana de la Discòrdia 134–135
Maremagnum 85, 100
Maritime Museum 88–89
markets 66–67
Mercat de la Boqueria 19, 66, 90
La Mercè 88
metro 11, 27
Miró, Joan 40–41, 150–151
Miró Foundation 40–41, 75
Modernisme 10, 76–77, 95, 129, 132, 134–135, 174
Monestir de Pedralbes 157
money 30
Montjuïc 42–43, 68, 74, 147
Montserrat 168–169
Monument a Colom 91
Museu d'Arqueologia, Barcelona 43
Museu d'Arqueologia, Girona 166, 167
Museu Arqueològic, Tarragona 178–179
Museu d'Art Contemporani de Barcelona (MACBA) 92–93
Museu de les Arts Decoratives 158

Museu de la Cera 69
Museu de Ceràmica 158
Museu de les Cultures del Vi de Catalunya 171, 172
Museu Egipci de Barcelona 137
Museu Etnològic 43
Museu Frederic Marès 93
Museu del Futbol Club Barcelona 68, 156
Museu d'Història de Catalunya 116–117
Museu d'Història de la Ciutat 94
Museu d'Història, Tarragona 179
Museu Maricel de Mar 175
Museu Marítim 88–89
Museu Nacional d'Art de Catalunya (MNAC) 44–45
Museu i Necropolis Paleocristians 179
Museu Picasso 19, 46–47
Museu Romàntic 175
Museu Tèxtil i d'Indumentària 158
Museum of Catalan History 116–117
Museum of Drawings and Prints 45
museum opening hours 32
music 111, 126, 146, 154, 161

national holidays 24
National Museum of Catalan Art 44–45
Nitbus 27
Numismatic Museum of Catalonia 45

Old City 87
Old Port 100
Olympic Games 120, 148–149
Olympic Ring 148–149
opening hours 32

Palace of Catalan Music 118–119
Palace of the Deputy 97
Palace of the Sea 116–117
Palau Güell 95
Palau de la Generalitat de Catalunya 99
Palau de Lloctinent 97
Palau de Mar 116–117
Palau de la Música Catalana 118–119, 126
Palau Reial Major 97
Palau Reial de Pedralbes 74, 158
Parc d'Atraccions del Tibidabo 69, 159
Parc de la Ciutadella 74, 120
Parc de la Creueta del Coll 74, 138
Parc de l'Espanya Industrial 74, 150
Parc de l'Estació del Nord 75
Parc de Joan Miró 75, 150–151
Parc del Laberint 75
Parc Zoològic 69
Park Güell 16, 48–49, 75
parks and gardens 74–75
Passeig Arqueològic, Tarragona 179
passports and visas 22
Pavelló Mies van der Rohe 151
Pedralbes district 155
El Penedès 170–173
personal safety 32
pharmacies 31, 32
Picasso, Pablo 16, 46–47
Picasso Museum 19, 46–47
Plaça de Catalunya 96
Plaça del Rei 97
Plaça Reial 67, 98
Plaça Sant Jaume 99
Les Platjas 114–115
Poble Espanyol 69, 152
police 31, 32
population 11
Port Olímpic 113, 120
Port Vell 100
postal services 30
public transport 27–28

rail travel 26, 27
Las Ramblas 16, 50–51, 85
La Ribera 54, 113, 114
rickshaws 70
Royal Palace of Pedralbes 158
Royal Shipyards 88–89

La Sagrada Família 16, 52–53
Sant Martí Sarroca 171
Sant Sadorní d'Anoia 171
Santa Maria del Mar 54–55
Sants 147
sardana 19, 39
seat belts 28
senior citizens 29
Serra de Collserola 159
shopping 32, 80–81, 107–111, 124–125, 142–145, 154, 160
Sitges 174–175
Spanish Village 152
speed limits 28
sport 71
street art 78–79
students/young travellers 29
swimming 71
sun protection 31

tapas 19, 60–61, 106–107, 123–124, 142, 153–154
Tàpies Foundation 130
Tarragona 176–179
taxis 28
Teatre-Museu Dalí 165
telephones 30–31
theatre 112
Tibidabo 155, 159
Tibidabo Amusement Park 159
time differences 23
tipping 30
Torre Agbar 138
Torre de Collserola 159
tourist offices 23, 29
Town Hall 99
trains 26, 27
trams 28
travelling to Barcelona 26–27

views 64–65
Vilafranca del Penedès 171, 172

walk
Barri Gòtic 72–73
watersports 71
websites 23
what's on when 24–25
wheelchair access 11
wines and wineries 15, 170–173

youth hostels 29

Acknowledgements

The Automobile Association would like to thank the following photographers, companies and picture libraries for their assistance in the preparation of this book.

Abbreviations for the picture credits are as follows – (t) top; (b) bottom; (l) left; (r) right; (AA) AA World Travel Library.

4l Parc Guell, AA/M Jourdan; **4c** Metro, AA/S L Day; **4r** Sagrada Familia, AA/P Wilson; **5l** Las Ramblas, AA/P Enticknap; **5c** Museu d'Historia de la Ciutat, AA/S L Day; **5r** Girona, AA/M Chaplow; **6/7** Parc Guell, AA/M Jourdan; **8/9** Sagrada Familia, AA/M Chaplow; **10/1t** Casa Mila, AA/S L Day; **10l** Barceloneta, AA/M Jourdan; **10r** Musician, AA/M Jourdan; **11c** Barri Gotic, AA S L Day; **11b** Sagrada Familia, AA/M Jourdan; **12/13** Mercat de la Boqueria, AA/M Jourdan; **12l** Olive oil, AA/S McBride; **12r** Mercat de Santa Caterina, AA/S McBride; **13** El Lobito restaurant, AA/S McBride; **14t** Casa Antigua, AA/M Chaplow; **14l** meal, Restaurant Salamanca, AA/S McBride; **15tl** Gracia market, AA/M Jourdan; **15cl** wine shop, AA/S McBride; **15r** wine bottles, AA/S McBride; **16** Sardana dancers, AA/S L Day; **17** Parc Guell, AA/M Jourdan; **18** Placa de Olles, AA/M Chaplow; **19t** Alpargatera from a sardana dancer, AA/M Bonnet; **19b** Mercat de la Boqueria, AA/S McBride; **20/1** Drassanes tube station, AA/S M Bonnet; **25** La Merce, AA/M Jourdan; **27** Barcelona Airport, AA/S L Day; **27** Metro sign, AA/M Jourdan; **28** Taxis, Port Olimpic, AA/S L Day; **31** Public telephone, AA/M Bonnet; **34/5** Sagrada Familia, AA/P Wilson; **36/7** Casa Mila, AA/S L Day; **36** Casa Mila, AA/M ChaplowBonnet – Courtesy of Caixa Catalunya; **38** Cathedral, AA/ M Chaplow; **38/9** Cathedral, AA/S L Day; **39** Cathedral, AA/M Jourdan; **40/1** Fundacio Joan Miro exterior with Quatre Ailes (1972), sculpture by Alexander Calder, Photo: AA/M Bonnet – © Calder Foundation, New York/DACS, London; **42/3** View from Castle Montjuic, AA/M Jourdan; **43t** Montjuic, AA/M Jourdan; **43b** Placa de la Font Magica, AA/M Jourdan; **44** Museu Nacional d'Art de Catalunya, AA/M Jourdan; **44/5** Museu Nacional d'Art de Catalunya, AA/M Jourdan; **45** Museu Nacional d'Art de Catalunya, AA/M Bonnet; **46cl** Museu Picasso, AA/M Chaplow; **46bl** Museu Picasso, AA/P Wilson; **47** Museu Picasso, AA/M Chaplow; **48r** Parc Guell, AA/S L Day; **48/9** Parc Guell, AA/M Jourdan; **49** Parc Guell, AA/M Jourdan; **50bl** Las Ramblas, AA/S L Day; **50br** Las Ramblas, AA/S L Day; **51** Las Ramblas, AA/M Bonnet; **52t** Passion Façade, Sagrada Familia, AA/M Jourdan; **52/3** Sagrada Familia, AA/M Jourdan; **53** Sagrada Familia, AA/P Wilson; **54** Santa Maria del Mar, AA/M Bonnet; **54/5** Santa Maria del Mar, AA/M Bonnet; **55** Santa Maria del Mar, AA/P Wilson; **56/7** Antigua Casa Figueras Café next to Las Ramblas, AA/M Bonnet; **58** Café scene, AA/S L Day; **61** Tapas selection, AA/T Carter; **62/3** Restaurant interior, AA/M Bonnet; **64/5** View toward Placa d'Espanya, AA/S L Day; **66/7** Mercat de la Boqueria, AA/S McBride; **69** L'Aquarium, AA/M Jourdan; **70/1** Goldondrina, AA/M Jourdan; **72** Ajuntament, AA/S L Day; **72/3** Barri Gotic, AA/M Bonnet; **75** Parc del Laberint, AA/M Chaplow; **76/7** Casa Mila, AA/S L Day; **78** Barcelona Head, AA/M Chaplow; **78/9** Dona i Ocell, AA/M Jourdan; **80/1** Shopping bag, AA/M Chaplow; **82/3** Palau de la Generalitat, AA/M Bonnet; **85** Las Ramblas, AA/M Jourdan; **86/7** Placa de Olles, AA/M Chaplow; **88** Musicians, AA/M Chaplow; **88/9** Drassanes and Museu Maritim, AA/M Jourdan; **90** Mercat de la Boqueria, AA/S McBride; **90/1** Columbus Monument, AA/S L Day; **92/3b** Museu d'Art Contemporani de Barcelona, AA/M Jourdan; **92/3c** Museu Frederic Mares, AA/M Bonnet; **94** Museu d'Historia de la Ciutat, AA/M Jourdan; **95** Palau Guell, AA/M Jourdan; **96/7** Placa de Catalunya, AA/S L Day; **97** Placa del Rei, AA/M Jourdan; **98** Placa Reial, AA/S L Day; **98/9** Placa Reial, AA/P Wilson; Palau de la Generalitat, AA/S L Day; **100** Maremagnum, AA/M Jourdan; **113** La Ribera, AA/M Chaplow; **114/5** Barceloneta esplanade, AA/M Bonnet; **115** Platja de la Barceloneta, AA/M Bonnet; **116** Palau de Mar, AA/M Jourdan; **116/7** Palau de la Mar, AA/M Chaplow; **119** Palau de la Musica Catalana, AA/M Jourdan; **120t** Parc de la Ciutadella, AA/M Bonnet; **120b** Vila Olimpica, AA/M Bonnet **127** Passeig de Gracia, AA/M Chaplow; **128/9** L'Eixample, AA/M Chaplow; **129** Farmacia Bolos, AA/M Chaplow; **130/1** Fundacio Antoni Tapies, AA/M Jourdan; **131t** Casa Vicens, AA/M Jourdan; **131b** Casa Vicens, AA/M Bonnet; **132** Hospital de la Santa Creu I Sant Pau, AA/M Jourdan; **133** Hospital de la Santa Creu I Sant Pau, AA/M Jourdan; **134** Casa Batllo, AA/M Bonnet; **135** Casa Lleo-Morera, AA/M Chaplow; **136/7** Parc Guell, AA/M Jourdan; **137** Museu Egipci, AA/M Bonnet; **138** La Sagrada Familia, AA/M Chaplow; **147** Cable car, Montjuic, AA/S L Day; **148/9** Anella Olimpica, AA/M Chaplow; **148** Palau Sant Jordi, AA/S L Day; **149** Caixa Forum, AA/M Bonnet **150/1** Parc de l'Espanya Industrial, AA/S L Day; **150br** Parc de Joan Miro, Dona i Ocell, AA/M Jourdan; **151** Pavello Mies van der Rohe;Photo: AA/M Bonnet – © Fundació Mies van der Rohe **152** Poble Espanyol, AA/M Jourdan; **155** Monestir de Pedralbes, AA/M Jourdan; **156t** Camp Nou, AA/M Bonnet; **156b** Camp Nou, AA/M Bonnet **157** Panels, Monestir de Pedralbes, AA/M Jourdan; **158** Palau Reial de Pedralbes, AA/M Bonnet – Courtesy of Museu de la Ceramica; **159** Parc d'Atraccions, AA/M Chaplow; **162/3** Girona, AA/M Chaplow; **165** Teatre-Museu Dali, AA/M Chaplow; **166** Girona, AA/M Chaplow; **166/7** Hostalric, Girona, AA/M Chaplow; **168** Montserrat, AA/M Bonnet; **169** Black Virgin statue, Montserrat, AA/S Watkins; **170/171** Coves Codorniu, AA/M Bonnet; **172/3** Vilafranca de Penedes, AA/P Wilson; **174/5** Sitges, AA/M Bonnet; **176** Tarragona, AA/P Enticknap; **177** Tarragona, AA/P Enticknap; **178/9** Cathedral, Tarragona, AA/P Enticknap.
Every effort has been made to trace the copyright holders, and we apologise in advance for any accidental errors. We would be happy to apply the corrections in the following edition of this publication.

Street Index

Abadessa Olzet, Carrer de l' **2B**
A de Torrelles, Carrer **11C**
Adolf Florensa, Carrer d' **1C**
A F Cambó **21J**
Agudells, Carrer dels **12B**
Agramunt, Carrer d' **8C**
Agudells, Carrer dels **11B**
A Guimerà, Carrer **5C**
A Saragossa, Carrer d' **4D**
Alaba, Carrer d' **24K**
Alacant, Carrer d' **5C**
Albigesos, Carrer **9C**
Alcalde de Móst, Carrer de l' **11E**
Alcalde de Zalamea, Carrer **11C**
Alcoi, Carrer d' **6A**
Alcolea, Carrer d' **2F**
Aldana, Carrer **18K**
Alegre de Dalt, Carrer de l' **10E**
Alexandre de Torrelles, Carrer d' **11C**
Alfambra, Carrer **1C**
Alfonso Comín, Plaça **8A**
Alfons XII, Carrer d' **7E**
Alí Bei, Carrer d' **21J**
Àliga, Carrer **14H**
A Llanas, Carrer d' **10C**
Almeria, Carrer d' **14G**
Almirall Aixada, Carrer **20M**
Almirall Cervera, Carrer **20M**
Almogàvers, Carrer dels **22J**
Alpens, Carrer d' **14H**
Alt de Gironella, Carrer **4C**
Alzina, Carrer **9D**
Amigó, Carrer d' **6E**
Ample, Carrer **2e**
Andalusia, Carrer **13G**
Andrea Dòria, Carrer d' **21M**
Angel Guimerà, Carrer d' **5C**
Angli, Carrer d' **4B**
Antequera, Carrer d' **10C**
Antoni de Capmany, Carrer d' **13G**
A Piferrer, Carrer d' **9A**
Aragó, Carrer d' **16G**
Arboç, Carrer **11B**
Arc del Teatre, Carrer de l' **19K**
Arenys, Carrer d' **10A**
Aribau, Carrer d' **19H**
Arimon Carrer d' **6C**
Aristides Maillol, Carrer **1E**
Arizala, Carrer d' **1E**
Arquitecte Sert, Carrer de l' **24L**
Astúries, Carrer d' **8E**
Ataülf, Carrer d' **3d**
Atenes, Carrer d' **7C**
Augusta, Via **4B**
Aurora, Carrer l' **18J**
Ausiàs Marc, Carrer d' **21H**
Autonomia, Carrer **15G**
Avenir, Carrer de l' **6E**
Àvila, Carrer d' **24K**
Avinyo, Carrer d' **3d**

Bacardí, Carrer de **1F**
Badajoz, Carrer de **24L**
Badal, Carrer de **13H**
Badalona, Carrer **2F**
Bagur, Carrer de **1F**
Bailèn, Carrer de **22J**
Balboa, Carrer **21L**
Balcells, Carrer **10D**
Baldiri Reixac, Carrer de **1D**
Ballester, Carrer, de **7C**
Balmes, Carrer de **7D**
Barcelona, Moll de **19L**
Baró de la Barre, Carrer del **9B**
Baró St Lluis, Carrer **11D**
Beat Almató, Carrer del **9B**
Bederrida, Carrer **3A**
Beethoven, Carrer **5E**
Begur, Carrer de **1F**
Bèjar, Carrer de **16H**
Bellesguard, Carrer de **6A**
Benavent, Carrer **1E**
Benedetti, Calle de **5A**
Benet Mateu, Carrer de **3C**
Berga, Carrer **8E**
Berguedà, Carrer **4E**
Berlín, Carrer de **3F**
Berlinès, Carrer **6C**
Bertran, Carrer de **7C**
Betànja, Carrer **9A**
Betlem, Carrer **8D**
Biada, Carrer **8D**
Bianco, Carrer d'en **2F**
Bigai, Carrer **6B**
B Català, Carrer **2A**
Bismarck, Carrer **11D**
B Mercadé, Carrer **7E**
Bogatell, Avinguda del **23K**
Bolívar, Carrer **8C**
Bolívia, Carrer **24H**
Bonanova, Passeig de la **4B**
Bonanova, Plaça de la **6B**
Bonaplata, Carrer de **4B**
Bonavista, Carrer **8F**
Boqueria, Carrer **2c**
Bordeta, Carrer de la **15H**
Bordeus, Carrer **4E**
Bori i Fontestà, Carrer **4D**
Born, Passeig del **21K**
Borrell i Soler, Carrer de **2B**
Bosch i Gimpera, Carrer de **2B**
B Pi, Carrer **14H**
Brasil, Carrer del **1F**
B Reixac, Carrer **1D**
Briz, Baixada de **8C**
Bruc, Carrer del **21J**
Bruniquer, Carrer de **9E**
Brusi, Carrer de **7D**
Brussel.les, Carrer **12D**
B Sivilla, Carrer **6B**
Buenaventura, Muñoz, Carrer **22J**
Buenos Aires, Carrer de **5E**
Buscarons, Carrer **7C**

Caballero, Carrer de **3F**
Cabanes, Carrer de **18K**
Cáceres, Carrer **1F**
Calàbria, Carrer de **17G**
Calaf, Carrer de **6D**
Calatrava, Carrer de **5C**
C Almera, Carrer **12C**
Calvet, Carrer de **6E**
Camèlies, Carrer de les **10D**
Camp, Carrer del **6C**
Camp d'En Vidal, Carrer **6E**
Canalejas, Carrer de **1F**
Can Baró, Avinguda **11D**
Canet, Carrer **4B**
Can Mora, Camí de **10C**
Can Toda, Riera de **10D**
Can Tunis, Passeig de **14M**
Canuda, Carrer **2a**
Capità Arenas, Carrer del **3D**
Caravel.la Niña, Carrer **4D**
Cardedeu, Carrer de **9B**
Cardedeu, Passatge de **9B**
Cardenal Vives i Tutó, Carrer **3B**
Cardener, Carrer del **9D**
Carders, Carrer **21K**
Cardó, Carrer **2F**
Carme, Carrer del **18J**
Carmel, Carretera del **10C**
Carmel, Rambla del **11B**
Carolines, Carrer **8D**
Carrenca, Carrer **5C**
Carreras i Candi, Carrer **1F**
Carretes, Carrer de les **18J**
Cartagena, Carrer de **12F**
Cascades, Passeig de les **15J**
Casp, Carrer de **20H**
Castanyer, Carrer **7B**
Castell, Avinguda del **16L**
Castellbisbal, Carrer **10A**
Castellnou, Carrer **4C**
Castellterçol, Carrer de **9B**
Casteràs, Carrer **1F**
Castillejos, Carrer de **11E**
Catalunya, Plaça de **20J**
Catalunya, Rambla de **20H**
Catedral, Avinguda **4B**
Cavallers, Carrer dels **1B**
Cerdanyola, Carrer **2F**
Cerignola, Carrer **5C**
Ceuta, Carrer de **10B**
Cid, Carrer del **19K**
Ciencies, Carrer de les **12B**
Cigne, Carrer del **7E**
Circumval-lació, Carretera de **13M**
Circumval-lació, Passeig de **22K**
Cister, Carrer del **7A**
Ciutat, Carrer **3d**
Ciutat de Balaguer, Carrer **6C**
Clos, Passatge **13J**
Còdols, Carrer de **2e**
Coll Alentorn, Carrer de **10A**
Colom, Passeig de **2f**
Com Benitez, Carrer del **1E**
Comercial, Carrer de **21K**
Comtal, Carrer **3a**
Comte Borrell, Carrer del **18J**
Comte d'Urgell, Carrer del **18G**
Comtes de Bell.lloc, Carrer dels **3F**
Conca de Tremp, Carrer **11C**
Concòrdia, Carrer de la **17J**
Consell de Cent, Carrer del **15G**
Consolat de Mar, Carrer **21K**
Constança, Carrer de **4E**
Constitució, Carrer de la **13G**
Copèrnic, Carrer de **6C**

Corral, Carrer del **14H**
Còrsega, Carrer de **4F**
Corts, Travessera de les **1E**
Corts, Carrer les **2E**
Costa, Carrer de la **8C**
Creu Coberta, Carrer de la **15G**
Cros, Carrer **14G**

Dàlia, Carrer de la **14H**
Dalmases, Carrer de **5B**
Dalt, Ronda de **1B**
Dalt, Travessera de **9D**
Daoiz i V, Carrer **1F**
Dènia, Carrer **7E**
Descartes, Carrer **6D**
Déu i Mata, Carrer de **3E**
Diagonal, Avinguda **1C**
Diluvi, Carrer **8E**
Diputació, Carrer de la **16H**
Doctor, Carrer del **15L**
Doctor Roux, Carrer del **4C**
Doctor Trueta, Carrer del **23K**
Dolors Monserda, Carrer **4A**
Dominguez i Miralles, Carrer **3B**
Dominics, Carrer dels **7A**
Dr Aiguader, Carrer del **21L**
Drassanes, Avinguda de les **19K**
Drassanes, Plaça de les **19L**
Dr Bové, Carrer del **11C**
Dr Cadevall, Carrer **12D**
Dr Carulla, Carrer del **4B**
Dr F Darder, Carrer del **2B**
Dr Ferran, Carrer **3D**
Dr Fleming, Carrer del **4D**
Dr Ibáñez, Carrer **3E**
Dr J Albarràn, Carrer **1B**
D R Vila, Carrer **4D**
Dulcet, Carrer **1B**
Duquesa, Carrer de la **3B**

E Augusta, Carrer d' **1E**
E Bargés, Carrer d' **3F**
E de Pinós, Carrer **3A**
Eduard Conde de Trinquet, Carrer d' **3C**
E Giménez, Carrer d' **3B**
Elisabets, Carrer **1a**
Elisa, Carrer d' **7C**
Elkano, Carrer d' **17J**
Emancipació, Carrer de l' **5B**
Enamorats, Carrer dels **24G**
En Blanco, Carrer d' **2F**
Encarnació, Carrer de l' **9E**
En Gignàs, Carrer d' **3e**
En Grassot, Carrer d' **10F**
En Molist, Carrer d' **10D**
Enric Granados, Carrer d' **19H**
Entença, Carrer d' **4E**
Equador, Carrer de l' **4F**
Ermengarda, Carrer d' **15G**
Escipió, Carrer d' **7C**
Escoles Pies, Carrer de les **5D**
Escorial, Carrer de l' **9E**
Espanya, Plaça d' **16H**
Espasa de Montevideo, Avinguda d' **3A**
Esperança, Carrer de l' **5B**
Esplugues, Carretera d' **1B**
Esteve Terradas, Calle **8B**
Europa, Carrer d' **3D**
Evarist Arnús, Carrer d' **2E**
Exèrcit, Avinguda de l' **1B**
Exposicio, Passeig de l' **16K**

F Alegre, Carrer **11D**
Farell, Carrer de **15H**
Farigola, Carrer de la **9B**
Fastenrath, Carrer **10A**
Fco Giner, Carrer **8F**
F del Coll, Carrer **10B**
Fedralbes, Avinguda de **2C**
Felipe de Paz, Carrer **1E**
Ferran Aguiló, Carrer de **5D**
Ferran, Carrer de **2c**
Ferran Puig, Carrer **8C**
Figols, Carrer **2E**
Finlàndia, Carrer **14G**
Fisas, Carrer **1E**
Florència, Carrer **12D**
Floridablanca, Carrer de **17H**
Flos i Calcat, Carrer **3D**
Folgueroles, Carrer **7B**
Fontcuberta, Carrer **3C**
Font de la Mulassa, Passeig de la **12C**
Font Florida, Carrer **14H**
F Pèrez Cabrero, Carrer **5D**
F Primo de Rivera, Carrer **2C**
França, Carrer de **11D**
Franca Xica, Carrer de la **16J**
Francesc Carbonell, Carrer **3C**
Francesc Macià, Plaça **5E**
Francoli, Carrer del **7D**
Fraternitat, Carrer **8F**
Freixa, Carrer de **5C**
F Valls i Taberner, Carrer **7C**

Galileo, Carrer de **2F**
Gandesa, Carrer de **3D**
Ganduxer, Carrer de **5D**
García Mariño, Carrer **7A**
Gas, Carrer del **22L**
Gaudi, Avinguda de **11F**
Gavà, Carrer de **14H**
Gayarre, Carrer **15G**
Gelabert, Carrer **4E**
General Mendoza, Carrer **9A**
General Mitre, Ronda del **4D**
Gènova, Carrer **12D**
Gignàs, Carrer d'En **3e**
Ginebra, Carrer de **21L**
Girona, Carrer de **21G**
Gironella, Carrer **4C**
Gleva, Carrer de la **7D**
Glòria, Baixada de la **8C**
Glòries Catalanes, Plaça de les **24H**
Gomis, Carrer de **8B**
Gósol, Carrer **4C**
Goya, Carrer **8E**
Gràcia, Passeig de **20H**
Gràcia, Travessera de **6E**
Gran de Gràcia, Carrer **8F**
Gran Via de Carles III **2E**
Gran Via de les Corts Catalanes **13H**
Gran Vista, Carrer de la **11C**
Guadiana, Carrer del **14G**
Guatlla, Carrer de la **14H**
Guillem Tell, Carrer **7D**
Guinardó, Ronda del **10D**
Guitard, Carrer de **3F**
Gustavo Bécquer, Carrer de **8B**

Hercegovino, Carrer **6C**
H Lázaro, Carrer **10E**
Homer, Carrer d' **8C**
Horaci, Carrer d' **6B**
Hort de la Vila, Carrer **4B**
Hospital, Carrer de l' **18J**
Hospital Militar, Avinguda de l' **8C**
Hurtado, Carrer **8B**

Icària, Avinguda d' **23L**
Igualada, Carrer **9F**
Ildefons Gerda, Plaça d' **13H**
Immaculada, Carrer de la **5A**
Independència, Carrer de la **12F**
Indústria, Carrer de la **9F**
Iradier, Carrer d' **5B**
Isabel II, Passeig **21L**

Jacquard, Carrer **2F**
J Balari, Carrer **5C**
J Bertrand, Carrer **5D**
J Càncer, Carrer **6A**
J Ciurana, Carrer **11D**
Jesús i Maria, Calle **7A**
J Gamper, Carrer **3E**
J Gari, Carrer **8A**
J Giralt, Carrer **21J**
J Iglesias, Carrer de **2C**
J Jover, Carrer **8B**
J Martorell, Carrer **15G**
Joan Blanques, Carrer **9E**
Joan Carles I, Plaça **8F**
Joan d'Alòs, Carrer de **1A**
Joan d'Austria, Carrer de **23L**
Joan de Borbó, Passeig de **21M**
Joan Güell, Carrer de **2E**
Joan Peiró, Plaça **3F**
Joan XXIII, Avinguda de **1D**
Joaquin Costa, Carrer **19J**
Jocs Florals, Carrer dels **14G**
Johann S Bach, Carrer **5D**
John F Kennedy, Plaça **7B**
Jordi Girona, Carrer de **1C**
Josep Carner, Passeig de **18L**
Josep Tarradellas, Avinguda de **4F**
J Piquet, Carrer **4B**
J Roig, Carrer **1E**
J Serrano, Carrer de **11C**
Judici, Carrer **21M**
Junta de Com, Carrer **19K**

Lafont, Carrer de **18K**
Laforja, Carrer de **6E**
la Granja, Carrer **9D**
Laietana, Via **4e**
L Antunez, Carrer **7E**
La Rambla **1e**
Larrard, Carrer de **9D**
L Cárdenas, Carrer **5D**
L de Grignon, Carrer **3C**
Legalitat, Carrer de la **9D**
Lepant, Carrer de **11F**
Lesseps, Plaça de **8D**
Leyva, Carrer de **15G**
Lincoln, Carrer de **7D**
Llançà, Carrer **16G**
Lleida, Carrer de **16J**
Lleó XIII, Carrer de **7B**
Llibertat, Carrer de la **8F**
Llorens i Barba, Carrer **11E**
Lluçà, Carrer de **2E**
Lluçanes, Carrer del **6A**
Llull, Carrer de **23K**
L M Vidal, Carrer **11B**
Londres, Carrer de **5F**
Loreto, Carrer de **5E**
Lugo, Carrer de **11B**

Madrazo, Carrer dels **6D**
Madrid, Avinguda de **1E**
Magalhaes, Carrer de **17J**
Magdalenes, Carrer **4b**
Maignon, Carrer **8C**
Major de Sarrià, Carrer **4B**

Mallorca, Carrer de **16G**
Manacor, Carrer de **7C**
Mandri, Carrer de **6C**
Manila, Carrer de **3C**
Manso, Carrer de **17J**
Manuel de Falla, Carrer **3C**
Manuel Girona, Passeig de **2C**
Maó, Carrer de **6B**
Marçal, Passatge de **13H**
Marc Aureli, Carrer **6D**
Marcel.lí, Carrer **12A**
Mare, Avinguda de la **2A**
Mare de Déu de la Salut, Carrer **9D**
Mare de Déu del Coll, Carrer de la **8C**
Mare de Déu del Coll, Passeig de la **9B**
Mare de Déu dels Angels, Carrer de la **10A**
Mare de Déu de Montserrat, Avinguda de la **11D**
Mare de Déu de Port, Carrer de la **13J**
Margarit, Carrer de **17K**
Margenat, Carrer de **4A**
Marià Cubí, Carrer de **6E**
Mari, Carrer del **12C**
Marina, Carrer de la **11F**
Marítim del Nova Icària, Passeig **23L**
Marítim, Passeig **21M**
Marmella, Carrer **8B**
Marquesa de Vilallonga, Calle de la **5B**
Marquès de Barberà, Carrer del **19K**
Marquès de Campo Sagrado, Carrer del **18J**
Marquès de Comillas, Avinguda del **14J**
Marquès de l'Argentera, Avinguda **21K**
Marquès de Mulhacén, Carrer del **2C**
Marquès de Sentmenat, Carrer del **3E**
Martí, Carrer de **9D**
Martí i Franquès, Carrer **1D**
Martí i Julià, Carrer **3D**
Mas Casanoves, Carrer del **11E**
Masferrer, Carrer **2D**
Maspons, Carrer **8E**
Massens, Carrer de **9D**
Mas Yebra, Carrer **7B**
Maternitat, Carrer de la **2E**
M Auxiliadora, Carrer de **4C**
M Bleach, Carrer **15G**
M de D del Pilar, Carrer **10B**
M de Foronda, Carrer **12B**
M de la Rosa, Carrer **8F**
Mediona, Carrer **9A**
Mejía Lequerica, Carrer **2E**
Melcior de Palau, Carrer **2F**
Melilla, Carrer **7A**
Menéndez y Pelayo, Carrer **1D**
Mercè, Carrer de la **3e**
Mercedes, Carrer **9C**
Mercedes, Rambla **9C**
Meridiana, Avinguda **23J**
Mestre Nicolau, Carrer **5E**
Metges, Carrer **21J**
Mèxic, Carrer de **15H**
Milà i Fontanals, Carrer **9F**
Milanesat, Carrer del **4C**
Mineira, Carrer de la **13H**
Minerva, Carrer **7F**
Miquel Angel, Carrer **1F**
Miracle, Carrer **2F**
Miramar, Avinguda de **16K**
Miramar, Passeig de **17K**
Miret i Sans, Carrer **1B**
Mistral, Avinguda de **16H**
Modolell, Carrer de **5D**
Moianès, Carrer del **14H**
Moles, Carrer les **4a**
Moli, Camí del **15L**
Moneders, Carrer dels **1B**
Monestir, Carrer del **2A**
Monistrol, Carrer **9F**
Montcada, Carrer **21K**
Monterols, Carrer **3B**
Montjuïc, Carretera de **16L**
Montjuïc, Passeig de **17K**
Montmany, Carrer de **9E**
Montnegre, Carrer **4E**
Montornès, Carrer **9B**
Montornès, Passatge **9B**
Monts, Carrer **19K**
Montseny, Carrer del **8E**
Montserrat Casanovas, Carrer de **12C**
Móra d'Ebre, Carrer de **9B**
Morales, Carrer **4E**
Mossèn Amadeu Oller, Carrer de **14H**
Mozart, Carrer **8F**
M Serrahima, Carrer **8D**
Muhlberg, Carrer de **11C**
Muntadas, Carrer **15G**
Muntaner, Carrer de **6F**
Murtra, Carrer de la **11B**
Musitu, Carrer de **7C**
M Vilomara, Carrer **12C**
Nàpols, Carrer de **10F**
Nena Casas, Carrer de la **4C**
Neptú, Carrer **7E**
Nicaragua, Carrer de **4F**
Nil Fabra, Carrer **8D**
Noguera Pallá, Carrer **14G**
Nou de la Rambla, Carrer **17K**
Nou de St Francesc, Carrer **2d**
Novell, Carrer de **2E**
Numància, Carrer de **3F**

Oliana, Carrer d' **7E**
Olivera, Carrer de l' **16J**
Olot, Carrer d' **9C**
Olzinelles, Carrer d' **14G**
Om, Carrer de l' **19K**
Or, Carrer de l' **8E**
Osi, Carrer d' **3B**

Padilla, Carrer de **11E**
Pàdua, Carrer de **7C**
Països Catalans, Plaça dels **3F**
Palaudàries, Carrer **18L**
Palau Nacional, Mirador del **15J**
Pallars, Carrer de **23J**
Paloma, Carrer de la **19J**
Palou, Carrer de **9A**
Pamplona, Carrer de **24K**
Panamà, Carrer de **2A**
Parcerisa, Carrer de **13H**
Parlament, Carrer **17J**
Pasqual i Vila, Carrer **1D**
Pasteur, Carrer de **11C**
Pau Alcover, Carrer de **4B**
Pau Casals, Avinguda **5E**
Pau Claris, Carrer de **21H**
Pau Ferran, Carrer **10B**
Pau Gargallo, Carrer **1C**
Pavia, Carrer de **1F**
P de la Creu **3B**
P de Montcada, Carrer **3A**
Pearson, Avinguda de **1A**
Pedrell, Carrer del **12B**
Pedro i Pons, Carrer de **2C**
Pelai, Carrer de **19H**
Pere Serafí, Carrer **8E**
Perill, Carrer del **8F**
Perla, Carrer la **8E**
Peu de la Creu, Carrer del **19J**
P Galdós, Carrer **8D**
P I Campanar, Carrer **12C**
Picasso, Passeig de **22K**
Pi I Margall, Carrer de **10E**
Pintor Fortuny, Carrer **1a**
Pi, Plaça de **2c**
Piquer, Carrer de **18K**
Pius XII, Plaça **2C**
Planella, Carrer dels **5A**
Planeta, Carrer **8E**
Plató, Carrer de **6D**
Poeta Cabanyes, Carrer **17K**
Polònia, Carrer **11D**
Polvorí, Carrer del **14J**
Pomaret, Carrer de **5B**
Pompeu Fabra, Avinguda **10C**
Portal de l'Angel, Avinguda **3b**
Portal Nou, Carrer **21J**
Portbou, Carrer **1E**
Portell, Carrer **10B**
Porto, Carrer de **12A**
Portolà, Carrer **8B**
P Pahissa, Carrer **1E**
Praga, Carrer de **11D**
Prat, Rambla del **8E**
Princep d'Asturies, Avinguda del **7E**
Princesa, Carrer de la **21K**
Pr Jordi, Carrer **16H**
Progrès, Carrer **8F**
Provença, Carrer de **4F**
Providència, Carrer de la **9D**
Puiggari, Carrer de **3F**
Puig IX, Carrer **18L**
Puigmartí, Carrer **8E**
Pujades, Carrer de **23K**
Pujades, Passeig de **22K**
Pujol, Carrer **6C**
Putget, Carrer del **7C**

Quatre Camins, Carrer dels **6A**
Quelxans, Carrer **11C**
Quevedo, Carrer **9E**

Rabassa, Carrer de **9D**
Radas, Carrer de **17K**
Rajolers, Carrer **2F**
Ramiro de Maeztu, Carrer **10D**
Ramon Rocafull, Carrer **11B**
Ramon Trias Fargas, Carrer de **23L**
Ramon Turró, Carrer de **23K**
Ramón y Cajal, Carrer **9E**
Raset, Carrer de **5C**
Raval, Rambla del **19K**
R Batlle, Carrer **4C**
R Bonnat, Carrer **5E**
R Calvo, Carrer **6B**
R d'Escuder, Carrer **1F**
R de Castro, Carrer **11E**
Rector Triadó, Carrer del **16H**
Rector Ubach, Carrer **6D**
Regàs, Carrer **7E**
Regomir, Carrer **3d**
Rei Martí, Carrer **14G**
Reina d'Aragó **2F**
Reina E de Montcada, Passeig **3B**

Reina M Cristina, Avinguda de la **16J**
Reina Victòria, Carrer **5D**
Rei, Plaça del **4c**
Remei, Carrer del **3D**
Repartidor, Carrer **9C**
Republica Argentina, Avinguda de la **8C**
Reus, Carrer **6B**
Ribes, Carrer de **22J**
Ricart, Carrer de **16J**
Riego, Carrer **15G**
Riera Alta, Carrer de la **18J**
Riera de Tena, Carrer **13G**
Riereta, Carrer de la **18J**
Rios, Carrer **7C**
Riu de l'Or, Carrer **3C**
Rius i Taulet, Avinguda de **15J**
R Miquel i Planas, Carrer de **3A**
Robador, Carrer **19K**
Robi, Carrer del **8D**
Robrenyo, Carrer de **3F**
Rocafort, Carrer de **4F**
Roger, Carrer de **1E**
Roger de Flor, Carrer de **10F**
Roger de Llúria, Carrer de **21H**
Roma, Avinguda de **16G**
Roman Macaya, Carrer **7A**
Rosari, Carrer del **4C**
Ros de Olano, Carrer **8E**
Roser, Carrer del **17K**
Rosés, Carrer de **2F**
Rosselló, Carrer del **4F**
Rossend Arús, Carrer **14H**
Roura, Carrer de **6A**
R Sensat, Carrer **24L**
Rubens, Carrer de **9B**

Sabino de Arana, Carrer **2D**
Sagrat Cor, Carrer **4A**
Sagués, Carrer de **6E**
Sagunt, Carrer de **13G**
Salvà, Carrer **17K**
Salvat Papasseit, Passeig de **22L**
Samaniego, Carrer **10A**
Sancho de Avila, Carrer **23J**
Sanjoanistes, Carrer **7D**
Santa Agata, Carrer **8D**
Santa Amèlia, Carrer de **3C**
Santa Anna, Carrer **2a**
Santa Carolina, Carrer **11E**
Santa Catalina, Carrer **2F**
Santa Fe de Nou Mexic, Carrer **5D**
Santa Joana d'Arc, Carrer **12B**
Santaló, Carrer de **6E**
Santa Madrona, Passeig de **16K**
Sant Antoni Maria Claret, Carrer de **9F**
Sant Antoni, Ronda de **18J**
Santa Otilia, Carrer **11B**
Santa Rosa, Carrer **8D**
Sant Carles, Carrer **21L**
Sant Crist, Carrer del **14G**
Sant Eudald, Carrer **9B**
Sant Fructuós, Carrer de **14H**
Sant Genis a Horta, Cami de **12A**
Sant Gervasi de Cassoles, Carrer **6B**
Sant Gervasi, Passeig de **7B**
Sant Jaume, Plaça de **3c**
Sant Joan Bosco, Passeig de **4C**
Sant Joan de la Salle, Carrer **6A**
Sant Joan, Passeig de **22H**
Sant Pau, Carrer de **18K**
Sant Pau, Ronda de **18K**
Sant Pere més Baix, Carrer **21J**
Sant Pere Mitjà, Carrer **21J**
Sant Pere, Ronda de **20H**
Sant Quinti, Carrer de **1F**
Sants, Carrer de **1F**
Santuari, Carrer del **10B**
Santuari Sant Josep de la Muntanya, Avinguda **9D**
Saragossa, Carrer de **7C**
Sardenya, Carrer de **10E**
Sarrià, Avinguda de **4D**
Secretari Coloma, Carrer del **10E**
Segimon, Carrer **11B**
Segura, Carrer del **13J**
Seneca, Carrer **7F**
Septimània, Carrer **7D**
Sepùlveda, Carrer de **17H**
Sèrbia, Carrer **12D**
Sicilia, Carrer de **10F**
Siracusa, Carrer **8E**
S Mundi, Carrer **4B**
Solá, Carrer de **3E**
Sor Eulàlia d'Anzizu, Carrer **1B**
Sors, Carrer de **9D**
Sostres, Carrer de **9C**
St Antoni, Carrer **2F**
St Cugat del Vallès, Carrer **9C**
St Elies, Carrer de **7D**
St Eusebi, Carrer de **7D**
St Germà, Carrer **15H**
St Gregori Taumaturg, Plaça **5D**
St Guillem, Carrer **7D**
St Hermen, Carrer **7D**
St Joaquim, Carrer **8E**
St Jordi, Carrer **1F**
St Lluis, Carrer de **9E**
St Magi, Carrer **8D**
St Marc, Carrer **7E**
St Màrius, Carrer de **6C**
St Medir, Carrer **1F**
St Miquel, Riera de **8E**
St Rafael, Carrer de **18K**
St Roc, Carrer **15H**
St Salvador, Carrer de **9D**
Sugranyes, Carrer de **1F**

Tallers, Carrer dels **19H**
Tamarit, Carrer de **17J**
Tànger, Carrer de **24J**
Tapioles, Carrer de **17K**
Taquígraf Garriga, Carrer del **3E**
Taquigraf Serra, Carrer **4E**
Tarragona, Carrer de **16H**
Tavern, Carrer de **6D**
T del Remei, Carrer **9B**
Telègraf, Carrer del **12D**
Tenerife, Carrer **11D**
Tenor Massini, Carrer del **2F**
Tenor Viñas, Carrer del **5E**
Teodora Lamadrid, Carrer **7B**
Teodor Roviralta, Carrer de **7A**
Terol, Carrer **8E**
Tetuan, Plaça de **22H**
T Flomesta, Carrer **1F**
Thous, Carrer de **11D**
Tibidabo, Avinguda del **7B**
Ticià, Carrer de **8A**
Tigre, Carrer de **19J**
Til lers, Passeig dels **2C**
Tinent Coronel Valenzuela, Carrer del **1C**
Tirso, Carrer **10B**
Toledo, Carrer **14G**
Topazi, Carrer **8D**
Tòquio, Carrer **2C**
Tordera, Carrer de **8F**
Torras i Pujalt, Carrer **6C**
Torrent d'En Vidalet, Carrer del **9E**
Torrent de l'Olla, Carrer del **8F**
Torrent de les Flors, Carrer **9E**
Torres, Carrer **8F**
Torrijos, Carrer **9E**
Trafalgar, Carrer de **21J**
Tres Senyores, Carrer **9D**
Tres Torres, Carrer de les **4C**
Trias i Giró, Carrer **1C**
Trilla, Carrer **8D**
Tuset, Carrer **7E**

Universitat, Plaça de la **19H**
Universitat, Ronda **19H**

València, Carrer de **16G**
Valero, Carrer dels **5D**
Valladolid, Carrer de **2F**
Valldoncella, Carrer **19H**
Valldoreix, Carrer **9C**
Vallespir, Carrer de **3F**
Vallfogona, Carrer **8E**
Vallirana, Carrer de **7C**
Vallmajor, Carrer de **5D**
Valseca, Carrer **11D**
Varsòvia, Carrer de **12D**
Veciana, Carrer **9A**
Vendrell, Carrer **7A**
Verdi, Carrer de **9D**
Vergós, Carrer dels **4C**
Viada, Carrer **8D**
Via, Ronda de la **13G**
Vico, Carrer de **5C**
Viladomat, Carrer de **5F**
Vila i Vilà, Carrer de **18K**
Vilamari, Carrer de **16H**
Vilamur, Carrer **3E**
Vilardell, Carrer **15G**
Villafranca, Carrer **9D**
Villarroel, Carrer de **6F**
Vint-i-sis de Gener, Carrer **15H**
Violant d'Hongria, Carrer **1E**
Viriat, Carrer de **3F**
Vista Bella, Carrer de **6A**

Watt, Carrer **15G**
Wellington, Carrer de **23L**

Xifré, Carrer de **12F**

Zamora, Carrer de **24K**

Questionnaire

Dear Traveler

Your comments, opinions and recommendations are very important to us. So please help us to improve our travel guides by taking a few minutes to complete this simple questionnaire.

Send to: Essential Guides,
MailStop 64, 1000 AAA Drive, Heathrow, FL 32746–5063

Your recommendations...

We always encourage readers' recommendations for restaurants, nightlife or shopping – if your recommendation is added to the next edition of the guide, we will send you a FREE AAA Essential Guide of your choice. Please state below the establishment name, location and your reasons for recommending it.

_____

_____

_____

_____

_____

Please send me AAA Essential _____

About this guide...

Which title did you buy?

_____ AAA Essential

Where did you buy it? _____

When? m m / y y

Why did you choose a AAA Essential Guide? _____

_____

_____

_____

Did this guide meet with your expectations?

Exceeded ☐ Met all ☐ Met most ☐ Fell below ☐

Please give your reasons _____

_____

_____

_____

continued on next page...

Were there any aspects of this guide that you particularly liked? _____

_____

_____

_____

_____

_____

Is there anything we could have done better? _____

_____

_____

_____

_____

_____

About you...

Name (Mr/Mrs/Ms) _____

Address _____

_____

_____ Zip _____

Daytime tel nos. _____

Which age group are you in?

Under 25 ☐ 25–34 ☐ 35–44 ☐ 45–54 ☐ 55–64 ☐ 65+ ☐

How many trips do you make a year?

Less than one ☐ One ☐ Two ☐ Three or more ☐

Are you a AAA member? Yes ☐ No ☐

Name of AAA club _____

About your trip

When did you book? m m / y y When did you travel? m m / y y

How long did you stay? _____

Was it for business or leisure? _____

Did you buy any other travel guides for your trip? Yes ☐ No ☐

If yes, which ones? _____

_____

Thank you for taking the time to complete this questionnaire.

All information is for AAA internal use only and will not be distributed outside the organization to any third parties.